New Initiatives on

International Cooperation in Criminal Justice

New Initiatives on
International Cooperation in Criminal Justice

First edition published by Seoul National University Press in 2012
7th printing 2022

Seoul National University Press
1 Gwanak-ro, Gwanak-gu, Seoul 08826, Republic of Korea
Tel: +82-2-880-5252
Fax: +82-2-889-0785
Home page: http://www.snupress.com
Facebook: @snupress1947
Instagram: @snupress
E-mail: snubook@snu.ac.kr

ISBN 978-89-521-1372-6 (93360)

For help on purchase from outside Korea, contact;
joongyukim@gmail.com +82-10-4901-3201
hckslj93@gmail.com +82-10-7108-3198

New Initiatives on

International Cooperation in Criminal Justice

Joon Gyu Kim

Cheol-Kyu Hwang

SNUPRESS
Seoul National University Press

PREFACE

It is a great honor for me to have this book published, as it is the fruition of my career as a prosecutor for thirty years, striving especially for international criminal justice.

15 years ago, I happened to give lectures on International Cooperation in Criminal Justice to judges and prosecutors from many countries who came to Korea to learn from our legal experience. Not that I was an expert on this issue but since there were very few Korean prosecutors who could give lectures in English, I got the chance thanks to the 3-year experience of working at the Korean Embassy in the U.S. This became the start of this book.

Continuing this lecture, I also gave the lectures to young lawyers for many years. My lectures grew broader in scope as my career had progressed to international affairs in the Ministry of Justice.

As a member of the Executive Committee and as Vice President of the International Association of Prosecutors (IAP), I have worked together and corresponded with many prosecutors worldwide. All these experiences opened my eyes and enabled me to look for better ways to enhance international cooperation. Consequently, I proposed and drafted the 'Asia-Pacific Convention for Cooperation in Criminal Justice' as an IAP Model Treaty, which was discussed at IAP for more than 2 years and was approved at the 4th World Summit of Prosecutors General, Attorneys General and Chief Prosecutors.

While being Prosecutor General, I had an ambition to develop a comprehensive guide for international cooperation in criminal justice based on my lectures. I asked my staff of international cooperation to supplement and elaborate the research materials, who joined me as the co-author Cheol-Kyu Hwang. He contributed to this book with years of experience working at the Permanent Korean Mission to the United Nations.

As a visiting scholar at UIUC Law College, after retiring from Prosecutor General, I was lucky to have time to reorganize my visions and complete my career-long research. I also had the chance to present the research to law professors in UIUC and later, to law students at the University of Chicago. This became the completion of this book.

This book, although not academically based, aims to figure out the ways to advance international cooperation against transnational crimes through case studies and field experience. It is my hope that this book will be used as a reference by prosecutors and law enforcement officers around the world. I wish this book to make a modest contribution to International Criminal Law. I also look forward to the day that the IAP Model Treaty of Asia-Pacific Convention proposed by myself would develop into the U.N. Regional Convention.

Finally, I would like to dedicate this first book of mine to my wife and two daughters, who have always stood by me and been on my side for my life.

Joon Gyu Kim

ACKNOWLEDGMENTS

This book would not have been possible without the support and contribution of many people. We would like to express our gratitude to everyone who has helped writing this book, sparing their own time from their busy lives.

First and foremost, we wish to thank Professor Charlotte Ku and Professor Jacqueline Ross, the advisors on this book for their encouragement and guidance for the direction of the research. Also, we would like to extend the gratitude to the Law Professors of UIUC for their warm hospitality during my stay.

We would like to thank Professor Jae-Chun Won, Prosecutor Hanjo Kim, Ms. Diane Goeun Kim, Mr. Wookyu Kim and Mr. Seong Beom Lee who aided with the follow-up research in data collecting and the preliminary undertaking based on my lectures. Additionally, we are grateful to Ms. Jin Young Kim, Ms. Ji Won In and others in UIUC who lent their hands extensively in revising the research.

We also benefited from the effort that Ms. Deokjoo Rah and Ms. Kayla Shinyoung Byun provided in the final editing and proofreading. Our special thanks goes to the Seoul National University, President Yeon-Cheon Oh, Professor Jae Hyung Kim, Professor Chongsuh Kim and the staff from the Seoul National University Press, for publishing and appreciating the merit of this book.

We owe our gratitude to the prosecutors worldwide who have joined the IAP, especially the Executive Committee members, who have worked together as colleagues for the international cooperation in criminal justice.

It was an honor to connect with all the Prosecutors General and the delegations who shared their valuable experiences and visions for the future of prosecution service at the 4th World Summit of Prosecutors General, Attorneys General, and Chief Prosecutors.

Finally, our heartfelt gratitude goes to those who have been with us during the process of this research and publishing.

Joon Gyu Kim

Cheol-Kyu Hwang

CONTENTS

INTRODUCTION

Traditionally, the criminal justice system focused on punishing crimes and prosecuting criminals locally. Over time, however, the role of prosecutors expanded, stretching into diverse dimensions including international matters.

'Transnational' is the most unique and popular trend in the 21st century. This expansion into the international realm is partly due to globalization and unprecedented technological developments. A natural development of this expansion has brought about an increase in trade and the movement of people, creating interdependence among countries. The dark side of such expansion, however, is the undesirable, yet inevitable, transnational development of crime.

Transnational crime has manifested itself in three ways.

First, there has been a growth of transnational characteristics in many crimes. Money-laundering is done on an international level. Drug trafficking is conducted across borders. Human trafficking and intellectual property infringement are increasing worldwide. Of course, cybercrime has no borders. Now many crimes, even those punished on domestic levels, are transnational in character.

Overall, crime has become elegantly organized and impressively sophisticated through the unprecedented use of information technology in the areas of recruitment and financing of criminal acts. In particular, criminal groups capitalize on the advancements in communication and transportation to expand their operations and form alliances across national borders.

Second, the number of crimes committed by foreigners in every country has increased. As the number of foreigners increases, it is only natural that the number of crimes committed by foreigners increases as well.

Third, there has been an increase in the number of suspects who escape overseas. This is the same for both foreigners and nationals in every country. The trends of expansion have made it easier for criminals to use national borders to protect themselves and to hide criminal evidence and profits from detection. Criminal networks take advantage of offshore centers to launder the proceeds of crimes and to seek safe havens in foreign jurisdictions.

Due to such internationalization of crime, law enforcement agents of every country face new difficulties. One difficulty is the overseas location of essential evidence. Another difficulty lies with the suspect's location beyond the reach of the territorial jurisdiction of the country.

Also, the lack of commonality among legal systems makes it more difficult to effectively counter transnational crimes.[1] Other problems that plague international cooperation include: an absence of enabling legislation, absence of channels of communication for the exchange of information, language barriers, procedural delays, insufficient law enforcement cooperation at the interregional level, and lack of training

---

1 For instance, within a relatively small geographical area such as Western Europe, the systems range from the inquisitorial to the adversarial, from common law to civil law. The significance of such legal variance entails different investigative and prosecutorial systems, which hinder law enforcement from attempting to work together across borders.

on effective means of making or granting cooperation requests.[2]

The Asia-Pacific region is certainly not exempted from this phenomenon.[3] Despite persistent efforts by many countries to resolve this issue, legal cooperation within the Asia-Pacific region has been underperforming, reflecting many problems and limitations.

This book proposes a direction for building stronger mechanisms and operations to achieve effective international cooperation. The twenty first century brings challenging problems with it. Those who are prepared and willing to overcome such obstacles, by connecting with and assisting each other, will not only overcome the challenges but will emerge as leaders who shape the future of law enforcement.

---

2 International cooperation requires money, personnel, and resources. Requesting countries may find that their cooperation requests are stalled as a result of a lack of infrastructure in the requested country. As such, relationships between law enforcement agencies of different countries are extremely difficult to establish. Such difficulties are widespread and affect every nation. Thus, there is a need for more effective, direct and speedy methods of international cooperation.

3 Tackling this issue has become a top priority as it challenges the integrity of the State and also threatens its security.

I. TRADITIONAL FRAMEWORK OF INTERNATIONAL COOPERATION

1. Legal Mechanisms

The two major difficulties that have become manifest due to the internationalization of crime are: (1) the suspect is located beyond the reach of the home country's territorial jurisdiction; and (2) essential evidence is located across borders and in foreign locations. There is widespread consensus that international cooperation is the most effective way to overcome these difficulties.[4]

International cooperation is largely achieved through legal mechanisms. Practitioners must be aware of such devices and apply them to cases. Actual use of these tools can take many different forms. This depends not only on the existence and contents of a valid international agreement, but also on the type of offence, the law and practice of a country.[5]

Two major legal mechanisms that have developed in response to

---

4 *See* Matti Joutsen, International Cooperation Against Transnational Organized Crime: Extradition and Mutual Legal Assistance in Criminal Matters at 364.

5 *Id.*

each of the difficulties mentioned above are 'extradition' and 'mutual legal assistance'[6] which will be further explored in this section.[7] Other possible areas of development in international cooperation include transfer of sentenced persons, asset recovery, and technical assistance.

These legal mechanisms are carried out through different types of arrangements. These include various domestic legislation, bilateral treaties, and multilateral treaties between countries.[8] A country can rely on one or more of these bases when seeking or providing cooperation, depending on the other country and type of assistance wanted.[9]

Bilateral treaties are formed when two countries have formally agreed on how they would handle matters requiring international cooperation between the two countries. Multilateral treaties are treaties in which many countries have agreed on how they would govern instances requiring international cooperation. Some advantages to treaty-based cooperation are that a treaty creates an obligation to cooperate under international law, provide greater certainty and clarity than most non-treaty based agreements, and provide forms of cooperation that would otherwise be unavailable.[10] Some disadvantage to treaties is that the negotiation process is time-consuming and costly, and it is impossible to sign a treaty with every country in the world.[11]

---

6 Hereinafter *MLA*.

7 Section III of this book will discuss actual cases that show these legal mechanisms in action.

8 OECD, Mutual Legal Assistance, Extradition and Recovery of Proceeds of Corruption in the Asia and the Pacific at 27.

9 *Id.*

10 *Id.*

11 Kimberly Prost, Breaking Down the Barriers: Inter-National Cooperation in Combating Transnational Crime at 7; OECD, *supra* at 27, 32.

One way to overcome these disadvantages is to cooperate without treaties based on domestic legislation.[12] When relying on domestic legislation, the law of the requested State is usually followed for sending, receiving, considering, and executing requests.[13] While this may be quicker and cheaper to implement, there is no obligation to cooperate under international law. In many cases, this kind of cooperation will only occur if the requested State agrees to reciprocity.[14]

Treaties can be written to focus on a single legal mechanism. For examples of such treaties on extradition and mutual legal assistance, one can look at the *Model Treaty on Extradition* and the *Model Treaty on Mutual Assistance in Criminal Matters* (*Model Treaties*). These treaties were carefully developed by the United Nations as a vehicle for international cooperation between all countries regardless of legal systems or legal backgrounds.[15] The purpose of the model treaties was to provide a suitable basis for negotiations between States that do not have such treaties. The model treaties are by no means a binding template. States can freely decide on any changes, deletions, and additions. We will use the text of these treaties when providing examples.

On the other hand, treaties can also be written to comprehensively cover many different kinds of legal mechanisms in one treaty. Two

12 OECD, *supra* at 32.

13 *Id.*

14 *Id.*

15 United Nations Office on Drugs and Crimes, Revised Manual on the Model Treaty on Mutual Assistance on Criminal Matters at 67[hereinafter *Revised Manual on MT on MA*].

prime examples would be the *United Nations Convention against Transnational Organized Crime* (UNTOC), also known as the Palermo Convention, and the *United Nations Convention against Corruption* (UNCAC). Not only do they both cover extradition and mutual legal assistance, there are clauses addressing proceeds of crime, protection of victims, and technical assistance among many other clauses.

Now, we will introduce extradition, mutual legal assistance, transfer of prisoners and the accompanying principles, which are often the key legal mechanisms for international cooperation.[16]

Extradition

Successful extradition can be seen through the *Nigerian Drug Dealer Case*

Extradition is the process by which a person charged with an offence is forcibly transferred to a State for trial, or a person convicted of an offence is forcibly returned to a State for the enforcement of punishment.[17]

When extraditing a person, the first issue is whether it is even possible to have him extradited.[18] Accordingly, there are various conditions and limitations that must be met before extradition can be granted. The exact conditions differ depending on the country and treaty.

For instance, offences eligible for extradition are often limited by

16 *See* OECD, *supra* at 25.

17 Joutsen, *supra* at 364.

18 Prost, *supra* at 3.

the double criminality requirement,[19] which dictates that the offence must be a crime in both States. Most extraditions are also limited to offences that are punishable by more than a year of imprisonment, or some other specified time set by the countries. These conditions would be laid out in the extradition treaty.

As such, an extradition treaty creates an obligation to extradite for extraditable offences as defined by the treaty. The obligation arises for the requested State once it receives the extradition request. The obligation is subject to the treaty provisions and applies to persons in relation to an extraditable offence.[20] The *UN Model Treaty* has an example text.

UN Model Treaty on Extradition
Article 1 – Obligation to Extradite

Each Party agrees to extradite to the other, upon request and subject to the provisions of the present Treaty, any person who is wanted in the requesting State for prosecution for an extraditable offence or for the imposition or enforcement of a sentence in respect of such as offence.

This clause is the fundamental basis of the *Model Treaty on Extradition*. It is the clause that creates the obligation to extradite for an extraditable offence.[21]

For a long time, neither domestic laws nor international treaties existed regarding the conditions or procedures of extradition. Bilateral

19 *See* Section I.2.

20 *Revised Manual on MT on MA*, *supra* note 15, at 7.

21 *Id.*

extradition treaties did not begin to emerge until the 1800's.[22] One of the first multilateral conventions was the influential *European Convention on Extradition* in 1957, still in force today.[23] In order to promote new extradition treaties and to provide guidance in their drafting, the United Nations prepared a *Model Treaty on Extradition* in 1990. In 2002, ensuring that the *Model Treaty* continues to reflect the most recent trends in extradition, the United Nations adopted the *Revised Manual on the Model Treaty on Extradition* prepared by an intergovernmental expert group commissioned by the United Nations.[24]

In addition to these general treaties on extradition, provisions on extradition have also been included in several international conventions that deal with specific subjects, such as UNTOC and UNCAC.

Mutual Legal Assistance (MLA)

MLA was successfully provided in the *Fled Rapist Case, Nigerian Drug Dealer Case*, and *Seorae French Village Infanticide Case*

The purpose of extradition is to get a foreign State to send a fugitive to the requesting State so that the fugitive can be placed on trial, or carry out their sentence. The purpose of mutual assistance, on the other hand, is to get a foreign State to assist in getting evidence.[25] This is important because all prosecutors need evidence to fulfill their

22 Joutsen, *supra* at 366.

23 *Id.*

24 *Revised Manual on MT on MA supra* note 15, at 4.

25 Joutsen, *supra* at 378.

duties.[26] Accordingly, mutual legal assistance can be defined as a process by which countries seek and provide assistance in gathering evidence for use in criminal cases.[27]

Mutual legal assistance allows for a wide scope of assistance between countries, in a direct and efficient manner. Assistance can be provided during any stage in the criminal process, from investigation to trial. This would include taking testimony or statement of persons for investigation or trial; providing documents, records, and articles of evidence; and serving documents such as summons or subpoenas. It also includes locating or identifying persons, transferring persons in custody for testimony, and executing requests for search and seizure.

The recent trend appears to be moving toward a constant expansion of this scope.[28] This can be seen below in the *Model Treaty for Mutual Assistance in Criminal Matters* when it calls for the widest possible measure of mutual assistance.

UN Model Treaty for Mutual Assistance in Criminal Matters
Article 1 – Scope of Application

1. The Parties shall, in accordance with the present Treaty, afford to each other the widest possible measure of mutual assistance in investigations or court proceedings in respect of offences the punishment of which, at the time of the request for assistance, falls within the jurisdiction of the judicial authorities of the requesting State.

The *Model Treaty* goes on to give an inclusive list of the types

26 Prost, *supra* at 11.

27 *Id.*

28 Joutsen, *supra* at 380.

of assistance available, rather than an exclusive list. On the list are: taking evidence or statements from persons, assisting in obtaining statements or evidence from detained persons or others, serving judicial documents, executing searches and seizures, examining objects and sites, providing information and evidentiary items, and providing relevant documents and records.

The history of mutual legal assistance treaties can be traced to the past few decades. One of the earliest examples was the *European Convention on Mutual Assistance in Criminal Matters*, which was developed by the Council of Europe in 1959 and is still being used today. The establishment of this convention signified the international community's recognition of the importance of having an instrument for cooperation in evidence-gathering among nations.[29] As such, mutual assistance is now generally based on bilateral or multilateral treaties. Over the years, some international treaties, such as the UNCAC or UNTOC, have been drafted to deal with specific offences. These instruments generally include extensive provisions on mutual legal assistance, as well as extradition.

Transfer of Sentenced Persons

Transfer of sentenced persons is a system in which a citizen of one country, who is serving one's imprisonment sentence in a foreign country, may be transferred to the country of citizenship to carry out

29 Prost, *supra* at 13.

the rest of the sentence. The purpose of a transfer back to the prisoner's home country is to help the person's social rehabilitation.

Generally, the sentenced person may express his interest at first in being transferred to either the sentencing State or to the administering State. Further, transfer may be requested by either the sentencing State or the administering State, normally through diplomatic channels. But, in special or emergency cases, diplomatic channels are not pursued and the transfer request can be filed directly to the central authorities.

Each country has its own procedure for the requests of the transfer of sentenced persons. However, consent of the sentenced person and the approval of both the sentencing and the administering States are basic conditions for the transfer of sentenced person. These conditions are stipulated in the statutes of each State. Similar to extradition, there are some other conditions that must be met before the transfer is possible, such as double criminality.

There is a widely known multilateral treaty for the transfer of sentenced persons. Currently being enforced, it is the Council of Europe's *Convention on Transfer of Sentenced Persons*. It has been ratified by sixty-four countries. Eighteen of the parties are outside of Europe, including the Republic of Korea, the United States, Japan, and Australia. The conditions of transfer in this particular treaty are as follows:

Council of Europe's Convention on Transfer of Sentenced Persons
Article 3 – Conditions for Transfer

1. A sentenced person may be transferred under this Convention only on the following conditions:
   a. If that person is a national of the administering State;
   b. If the judgment is final;
   c. If, at the time of the receipt of the request for transfer, the sentenced person still has at least six months of the sentence to serve or if the sentence is indeterminate;
   d. If the transfer is consented to by the sentenced person, or where in view of his age or his physical or mental condition one of the two States considers it necessary, by the sentenced person's legal representative;
   e. If the acts or omissions on account of which the sentence has been imposed constitute a criminal offence according to the law of the administering State or would constitute a criminal offence if committed on its territory; and
   f. If the sentenced and administering States agree to the transfer.

2. Basic Rules

International criminal law is a subset of international law and thus, derives its powers from the same basic sources as international law: treaties, international customs, and general principles. A few basic rules that are common in international cooperation are as follows:

Basic Rules of International Cooperation
Principle of Reciprocity
Principle of Double Criminality
Principle of Specialty

Next, we shall take a look at each of these principles and see how they affect extradition and mutual legal assistance in particular.

Principle of Reciprocity

Reciprocity is a promise by the requesting State that it will provide the same type of cooperation to the requested State in a same or similar case in the future.[30]

You can see the principle at work if you imagine the relationship between you and your neighbors. If you ask your next door neighbors for help in moving your furniture, you would likely get the following responses:

Friendly relation → "O.K., I will give you a hand."

No acquaintance → "No, I'm sorry."

→ "Yes, if and only if you give me the same help when I am in need."

The same rule applies to the international society. If one State were to ask for mutual legal assistance of another State, you would be likely to get the following responses:

Treaty in place → "No problem."

No treaty in place → It requires a guarantee of reciprocity.

Thus, if there is a treaty in place between the two States at the time of the request, the request can be granted on the condition of the treaty. But, if there is no treaty between the two States at the time of request, the requested State may require a guarantee of reciprocity before honoring the request. In practice, guarantee of reciprocity would be in the form of a diplomatic verbal note from the ambassador of the requesting country.

This principle governs treaties on both extradition and MLA. Both *Model Treaties* implicitly embody this principle rather than expressly stating it.

---

30 *See* OECD, *supra* at 25.

UN Model Treaty for Mutual Assistance in Criminal Matters
Article 1 – Scope of Application

The Parties shall, in accordance with the present Treaty, afford to each other the widest possible measure of mutual assistance in investigations or court proceedings...

By agreeing to provide the widest possible measure of mutual assistance to the other party, each side is inherently promising to reciprocally give and receive similar assistance.

Although it is a basic principle of international law, the current trend is moving away from requiring reciprocity.[31] For instance, the *Model Treaty for Mutual Assistance in Criminal Matters* recommends that parties permit mutual assistance without a treaty or reciprocity in its Commentary regarding the scope of mutual assistance.

UN Model Treaty for Mutual Assistance in Criminal Matters
Annex 2, Chapter 2

The model legislation should provide a full range of flexible options for assuming mutual assistance obligations. When there is a treaty on mutual assistance in criminal matters, the terms of that treaty should govern the relationship. The legislation should also permit mutual assistance to be provided without a treaty, with or without reciprocity.

---

31 Unlike extradition or mutual legal assistance, the principle of reciprocity does not apply to 'transfer of sentenced persons.' Transfer of sentenced persons is always executed based on treaties or conventions.

Principle of Double Criminality

Double criminality is defined as an act which constitutes a crime according to the laws of both States. There is an internationally recognized rule of mutual punishment based on *Nulla Crimen Sine Lege*[32]– the Principle of Legality of the Crime.[33]

Although this seems like a simple requirement, in practice, it becomes difficult to interpret due to the technical differences in how States define, name, and prove offences. For example, while one State calls the offence in question larceny, another may call it theft.[34] In this respect, we must ask the question of how to determine whether one clause of criminal code of one country matches another.

Traditionally, this was done by requiring the matching of the names or definitions of the applicable crimes. This technical approach led to many difficulties. Now, a more modern approach is to question whether the conduct is criminal in both States, regardless of the different names or elements. Thus, modern treaties provide detailed standards of whether the criminal conduct would be considered a criminal offence in both countries.

Generally, extradition treaties require that the offence in question be a crime according to the laws of both the requesting and the

32 No crime, no punishment.

33 Principle of Legality refers to a principle that a person may not be prosecuted under a criminal law that has not been previously published. When applied here, it means that there can be no extradition without a crime under the law of the requested State. Otto Lagodny, *Expert Opinion for the Council of Europe on Questions Concerning Double Criminality* at 3.

34 Prost, *supra* at 8.

requested State, and often also require that the offence carry a certain minimum punishment, such as imprisonment for one year or more. An example of such a clause can be found here:

UN Model Treaty on Extradition
Article 2, Paragraph 1 – Extraditable Offences

For the purposes of the present Treaty, extraditable offences are offences that are punishable under the laws of both Parties by imprisonment or other deprivation of liberty for a maximum period of at least [one/two] year(s), or by a more severe penalty...

Even where a State allows extradition in the absence of an extradition treaty, this principle of double criminality is generally applied.[35]

When applied to mutual legal assistance, the principle of dual criminality is less commonly required because MLA covers a broad spectrum of criminal investigations and information gathering. On the other hand, extradition has a narrower focus because it deals with offenders either convicted or charged by the criminal code of a specific country.

Although double criminality is a universal principle, there is a new trend to overcome its limits. Commentaries on both *Model Treaties* have clauses recommending that contracting States consider honoring requests even in the absence of dual criminality as seen below:

---

35 Joutsen, *supra* at 366.

UN Revised Manual on the Model Treaty on Extradition
Article 4, Paragraph 1, Footnote

Countries may wish, where feasible, to render assistance, even if the act on which the request is based is not an offence in the requested State (absence of dual criminality). Countries may also consider restricting the requirement of dual criminality to certain types of assistance, such as searches and seizure.

Principle of Specialty

Limitation on Use
Safe Conduct

In extradition, the widely-recognized international principle of specialty limits the power that the requesting State has over the person surrendered.[36] This rule places a limitation on the punishment or prosecution of the person who has been extradited. This means that the extradited person will only be prosecuted and punished for the offence in the request and not for other offences committed before the extradition, without prior consent of the requested State.[37]

An example of this principle can be found in the *UN Model Treaty on Extradition*:

UN Model Treaty on Extradition
Article 14 – Rule of Specialty

1. A person extradited under the present Treaty shall not be proceeded against, sentenced, detained, re-extradited to a third State, or subjected to any other restriction of personal liberty in the territory of the requesting State for any offence committed before surrender other than:
   (a) An offence for which extradition was granted
   (b) Any other offence in respect of which the requested State consents…

36 UN Model Treaty on Extradition at 52 (A/RES/45/116).

37 Black's Law Dictionary, Doctrine of Specialty, 2009.

The principle of use limitation is analogous to the principle of specialty but applies to MLA.[38] It places a limitation on the scope of the use of evidence obtained under the request. The evidence cannot be used for a purpose other than for those stated in the request, without prior consent of the requested State.[39] An example of this principle can be found in the *UN Model Treaty for Mutual Assistance in Criminal Matters*:

UN Model Treaty for Mutual Assistance in Criminal Matters
Article 8 – Limitation on Use

Unless otherwise agreed, the requesting State shall not, without the consent of the requested State, use or transfer information or evidence provided by the requested State for investigations or proceedings other than those stated in the request.

This principle also places a limitation on the punishment and prosecution of the person who has been transferred for testimony by request. Safe conduct is provided to persons transferred to take testimony in the requesting State with respect to any act or conviction which preceded the person's departure from the territory of the requested State. Crimes subsequently committed in the requesting State, such as perjury, can be prosecuted.

38 UN Model Treaty for Mutual Assistance in Criminal Matters at 99; OECD, *supra* at 49.

39 In the *Nigerian Drug Dealer Case*, the court records from Denmark were used solely for the purpose of prosecuting the criminal.

3. Grounds for Refusal

The decision to grant assistance depends on the requested State's legal framework, as well as its willingness to cooperate. In principle, international standards establish that the grounds for denying requests should be kept minimal and should only be exercised sparingly. In practice, however, there are varying limitations that provide for many grounds for refusal and make it difficult to obtain speedy assistance.

Generally when extradition requests are denied, there are two kinds of denial: mandatory denial and discretionary denial. Mandatory denial includes requests that relate to political offences, requests where the statute of limitations has run, and requests that relate to double jeopardy considerations, lack of evidence, and human rights considerations. Discretionary denial includes requests related to nationals, territorial jurisdiction, sovereignty considerations, double jeopardy in a third country and humanitarian considerations. The *UN Model Treaty on Extradition* provides the following lists as grounds for refusal:

UN Model Treaty on Extradition, Article 3 Mandatory Grounds for Refusal	**UN Model Treaty on Extradition, Article 4 Optional Grounds for Refusal**
• Political offence • Prejudice (race, religion, ethnic origin, nationality, etc.) • Military offence • *Nos bis in idem*/Double jeopardy • Lapse of time or other immunity from prosecution • Torture, cruel, inhumane, or degrading treatment or punishment and minimum guarantees in criminal proceedings • Judgment rendered in absentia • Further grounds (insufficient proof, *prima facie*)	• Nationals • Requested State declining to prosecute • Pending prosecution for the offence for which extradition is being requested • Death penalty • Extraterritoriality • Claim of requested State to jurisdiction over the offence • Extraordinary or *ad hoc* tribunal • Humanitarian exception

Unlike the *Model Treaty on Extradition*, the *Model Treaty for Mutual Assistance in Criminal Matters* does not have any mandatory grounds for refusal. A possible explanation is that mandatory grounds would be unnecessary as mutual assistance does not affect a person's liberty directly as much as extradition. As such, they included the following illustrative list of discretionary grounds in the *Model Treaty* that countries could rely on to refuse a request when appropriate:

UN Model Treaty for Mutual Assistance in Criminal Matters Article 4 – Refusal of Assistance
• Prejudice essential State interests • Political offence • Prejudice (race, religion, ethnic origin, nationality, etc.) • *Nos bis in idem*/Double jeopardy • Compulsory measures inconsistent with requested State's law and practice • Military offence

Next, we will take a closer look at some of the grounds for refusal of international cooperation, which are more commonly used.

Political Offence

A requested State may deny a request for mutual legal assistance or extradition, if it determines that the request is related to a political offence. However, there is no general consensus on the definition of a political offence in the international community. In deciding whether an offence qualifies as political, references are generally made to the motive and purpose of the offence, the circumstances in which it was committed, and whether the offence constitutes treason or sedition under domestic law. An example clause can be found in the *Model Treaty on Extradition*:

UN Model Treaty on Extradition
Article 3 – Mandatory Grounds for Refusal

Extradition shall not be granted in any of the following circumstances:
(a) If the offence for which extradition is requested is regarded by the requested State as an offence of a political nature.

Recent trends suggest that attempts are being made to restrict the scope of this exception or even to abolish it.[40] This is the case between the European Union countries. UNTOC does not make specific reference to political offences as grounds for refusal, even though it

40 Joutsen, *supra* at 371.

was listed as a mandatory ground for refusal in the *Model Treaty on Extradition* adopted only ten years earlier.

One factor that contributes to the limiting of the political offence exception is the growth of terrorism. If the offence is serious, such as murder, political terrorism, or genocide, courts in different countries have a tendency not to apply the political offence exception.[41]

Human Rights Considerations

Similar to the political offence limitation, a requested State may deny a request for extradition or mutual legal assistance if there are substantial grounds to believe that compliance with the request would facilitate the prosecution or punishment of a person on account of his race, religion, nationality, ethnic origin, sex, status, etc. If it is determined that the request was based on any of these characteristics upon examination of the request, the requested State does not need to render assistance.

The extradition of nationals was all denied in the *English Instructor Murder Case*, *Fled Rapist Case*, and *Seorae French Village Infanticide Case*.

Non-Extradition of Nationals

In general, States have long been willing to extradite nationals of the requesting State or of a third-party State. When it comes to extraditing their own nationals, however, most States have traditionally

41 *Id.* at 372.

refused to do so. This is likely because of an obligation to protect their citizens, lack of confidence in the fairness of foreign legal proceedings, and many disadvantages of defendants in a foreign legal system or foreign custody. Such a principle is usually expressly stated in treaties. An example clause can be found in the *Model Treaty on Extradition*:

UN Model Treaty on Extradition
Article 4 – Optional Grounds for Refusal

Extradition may be refused in any of the following circumstances:
(a) If the person whose extradition is requested is a national of the requested State.

However, the recent trend in extradition has been moving away from this previously strict rule. Some extradition treaties have provisions where a State can extradite its own national under various conditions. For example, under UNTOC, a State may extradite its own national on the condition that he or she is returned to serve out the sentence. Such a guarantee that the actual enforcement of any punishment would take place in the person's home country can be helpful in overcoming a State's reluctance to extraditing its own nationals. Another condition can be found in the *Model Treaty on Extradition*, where if extradition is refused on this ground, the requested State shall prosecute the person for the offence for which extradition had been requested, if the other State so requests.

The United States, the United Kingdom, and most other common law countries are willing to extradite their own nationals as long as there is a treaty.[42] This may have been due in part to the fact that these States have been less likely than civil law countries to assert jurisdiction over offences committed by their citizens abroad.[43] Thus, failing extradition, the offender would not be brought to justice at all.

Danger of Persecution

Recently, the rights of individuals have been increasingly regarded as the subject of international law. This has perhaps been most evident in extradition proceedings. In light of strengthening international human rights law, many of the more recent treaties pay particular attention to the nature of the proceedings and the expected treatment of the individual in the requesting State.

An example clause can be found in the *Model Treaty on Extradition*:

UN Model Treaty on Extradition
Article 3 – Mandatory Grounds for Refusal

Extradition shall not be granted in any of the following circumstances:

(f) If the person whose extradition is requested has been or would be subjected in the requesting State to torture or cruel, inhuman or degrading treatment or punishment or if that person has not received or would not receive the minimum guarantees in criminal proceedings…

42 UNAFEI, Refusal of Mutual Legal Assistance or Extradition at 190; Joutsen, *supra* at 369.

43 Joutsen, *supra* at 369.

State Interests

Generally speaking, treaties for mutual legal assistance in criminal matters provide that the requested State may refuse assistance which it deems might endanger its sovereignty, security, law and order, or other vital interests. This is a well-established ground for refusing to provide legal assistance that provides substantial protection for the countries.[44] For example, the *Model Treaty for Mutual Assistance in Criminal Matters*, UNCAC and UNTOC have provisions by which the requested State may refuse to grant mutual legal assistance if it considers that execution of the request is likely to prejudice its sovereignty, security, ordre public, or other essential interests.

On the other hand, refusing extradition on these grounds is less common, although some countries have included them in extradition treaties.[45] The *Model Treaty for Extradition*, however, has no mention of essential State interests in its lists of mandatory or discretionary refusal grounds.

Further Grounds for Refusal

Other than the more commonly used grounds for refusal that were introduced above, there are other grounds for refusal of international

44 Joutsen, *supra* at 37.

45 *See* OECD, *supra* at 50.

cooperation. Some other possible grounds provided by the *Model Treaty on Extradition* are as follows:

(a) if the act is only an offence under military law and not ordinary criminal law (Article 3);

(b) if the final judgment has already been rendered (Article 3);

(c) if the person is immune from prosecution or punishment for any reason (including lapse of time or amnesty) (Article 3);

(d) if the person would be subjected to torture or cruel, inhumane or degrading treatment (Article 3);

(e) if the person has received an unfair trial (including a finding of insufficient proof) (Article 3);

(f) if the requested State has decided either not to institute or to terminate proceedings against the person (Article 4);

(g) if there is pending prosecution for the offence (Article 4);

(h) if the person would receive the death penalty according to the laws of the requested State (Article 4);

(i) if the offence has been committed outside the territory of either party and the law of the requested State does not provide for jurisdiction over the offence (Article 4);

(j) if the requested State claims territorial jurisdiction over the offence (Article 4);

(k) if the person has been or is liable to be tried in the requesting State by an extraordinary or *ad hoc* court or tribunal (Article 4); or

(l) if the requested State thinks under the circumstances of the case, extradition would be incompatible with humanitarian considerations in view of age, health, or other personal circumstances of that person (Article 4).

It is noteworthy that the *UN Model Treaty on Extradition* treats death penalty as one of the grounds for refusal.

Some other possible grounds that mutual assistance might be denied, as provided by the *Model Treaty for Mutual Assistance in Criminal Matters*, are as follows:

(a) if the assistance requested is inconsistent with law and practices of the requested State (Article 4);

(b) if prosecution of the offence would be double jeopardy (Article 4).

II. CONTEMPORARY FRAMEWORK OF INTERNATIONAL COOPERATION

1. International Activities

International cooperation in criminal matters has come to new stage. Notable examples of international organizations in the field of legal cooperation include the UNODC, the international tribunals, and the International Association of Prosecutors. Furthermore, most of the regions in the world have developed formal communication networks between legal institutions. Such is the case in Europe with the establishment of Eurojust and its affiliated judicial network (EJN), or in South America with the *Ibero*-American Assistance network (IberRed).

International Organizations

UNODC

Established in 1997, the United Nations Office on Drugs and

Crime (UNODC)[46] works to educate the world about the dangers of drug abuse and to strengthen international action against drug production, trafficking, and drug-related crimes. In order to achieve this, UNODC carries out a broad range of initiatives, including alternative development projects, illicit crop monitoring and anti-money laundering programs.

UNODC contributes to improve crime prevention and to assist with criminal justice reform in a number of countries. The office works with Member States to strengthen the rule of law, promote stable and viable criminal justice systems and combat the growing threats of transnational organized crime and corruption.[47]

International Tribunals

The International Criminal Court (ICC),[48] governed by the Rome Statute, is the first permanent treaty-based international criminal court. It was established to help end the impunity of perpetrators of the most serious crimes which are a matter of concern to the international community. The ICC is an independent international organization, and is not part of the United Nations system.

The ICC has a permanent status unlike the ad hoc criminal courts established by the United Nations Security Council, such as the International Criminal Tribunal for the former Yugoslavia (ICTY) and

46 www.unodc.org

47 The UNODC also resolved to help Korea in preparations for the 4th World Summit of Prosecutors General held in June 2011 in Seoul, Korea.

48 www.icc-cpi.int

the International Criminal Tribunal for Rwanda (ICTR).[49] In all of its activities, the ICC relies on international cooperation, in particular from various States. State Parties are obliged to cooperate fully with the ICC in its investigations and prosecutions. State Parties may cooperate in, *inter alia*, arresting persons wanted by the ICC, providing evidence for use in proceedings, relocating witnesses, and enforcing the sentences of convicted persons. The ICC may also receive cooperation from non-State Parties, and may enter into arrangements or agreements to provide cooperation.

Networks

International Association of Prosecutors

The International Association of Prosecutors (IAP),[50] which is a non-governmental and non-political organization, is the only worldwide association of prosecutors. The establishment of such an organization was required to cope with the rapid growth in transnational crimes. Thus, the IAP was established in June 1995 in the United Nations offices in Vienna.

The IAP aims to promote effective, fair, impartial, and efficient prosecution of criminals and to assist prosecutors internationally in

---

49 Because these tribunals were established to try crimes committed only within a specific time-frame and during a specific conflict, a general agreement for the need of an independent, permanent criminal court arose.

50 www.iap-association.org

the fight against organized or other serious crimes. For that purpose, it promotes international cooperation in gathering and providing evidence; in tracking, seizing and forfeiting the proceeds of serious crime; and in the prosecution of fugitive criminals.

Its website provides much information for prosecutors with an active interest in other jurisdictions. Members can access certain specialized sites, including the Global Prosecutors E-Crime Network (GPEN), the Forum for International Criminal Justice (FICJ), as well as contact points in other countries which can prove to be essential when dealing with cross-border criminality.

The signature event of IAP is the Annual Conference. The 16th Annual Conference was held in Korea in 2011, side by side with the 4th World Summit of Prosecutors General, Attorneys General and Chief Prosecutors.

Eurojust

Eurojust[51] is the European Union (EU) judicial cooperation unit. Eurojust was formally established in 2002 to improve the effectiveness of national competent authorities within the EU in investigating and prosecuting cases of serious cross-border crimes. Eurojust is comprised of 25 national members, known collectively as the College, which also acts as the management board of the organization. The national members nominated experienced judges, prosecutors, or police officers of similar competence to work together as a permanent network in

---

51 www.eurojust.europa.eu

Eurojust's premises in The Hague, Netherlands.

Eurojust's key objective is to ensure that serious cross-border crime is dealt with as effectively as possible by the EU member States. Therefore, Eurojust encourages, facilitates, and supports investigating and prosecuting authorities to work together. By coordinating their activities and assisting them to cooperate together, justice can be administered in a faster manner.

Eurojust has given high priority to its work in the fight against terrorism, but it is also involved in cases of human and drug trafficking, serious fraud and money laundering. Eurojust also has the responsibility to ensure that the existing mutual legal assistance, extradition treaties, and conventions operate efficiently.

European Judicial Network

The European Judicial Network (EJN)[52] is a network of national contact points for the facilitation of judicial cooperation in criminal matters between member States of the European Union. National contact points are designated by each member State among central authorities in charge of international judicial cooperation in serious crimes such as organized crimes, corruption, drug trafficking or terrorism. The Network is composed of more than three hundred national contact points from twenty seven EU member States,[53] the

52 www.haguejusticeportal.net

53 Austria, Belgium, Bulgaria, Cyprus, Czech Republic, Denmark, Estonia, Finland, France, Germany, Greece, Hungary, Ireland, Italy, Latvia, Lithuania, Luxemburg, Malta, Netherlands, Poland, Portugal, Romania, Slovakia, Slovenia, Spain, Sweden, and United

European Commission, and a Secretariat based in The Hague.

Contact points promote judicial cooperation between competent local authorities for the purpose of, for example, the dispatch and implementation of requests for judicial assistance as well as the establishment of the most appropriate direct contacts. In addition, contact points can help in resolving difficulties arising from the implementation of such requests.

Secretariat of the Network forms part of Eurojust but functions as a separate unit. It enjoys autonomy, as stated in the Council Decision[54] on the strengthening of Eurojust.

Ibero-American Legal Assistance Network

IberRed,[55] or the Ibero-American Legal Assistance Network, is a structure formed by the Latin American Community of Nations. *IberRed* was formed by the contact points from the Ministries of Justice and Central Authorities, Prosecutors and Public Prosecutors, and judicial branches of twenty three member countries.[56] The Network is aimed at optimizing instruments for civil and criminal judicial assistance and strengthening cooperation between countries.

Kingdom.

54 2008/426/JHA

55 www.unodc.org/international-cooperation-networks

56 Argentina, Bolivia, Brazil, Colombia, Costa Rica, Cuba, Chile, Dominican Republic, Ecuador, El Salvador, Guatemala, Honduras, Mexico, Nicaragua, Panama, Paraguay, Peru, Portugal, Puerto Rico, Spain, Uruguay, and Venezuela.

2. Emerging Trends

General Trends

In the practice of extradition and mutual legal assistance, gradual changes are being noticed. First of all, direct communication and simplified procedure have taken form, as procedural requirements have become less rigid when making requests for cooperation. Second, in order to effectively respond to the current aspect of transnational crimes, bilateral treaties are being replaced by multilateral treaties step by step.

Third, a clear tendency toward eliminating many refusal grounds for extradition or legal assistance could be found. An increasing number of States are allowing the extradition of their own nationals,[57] and refusal based on political offence is gradually diminishing.

Lastly, MLA measures have steadily expanded. At first, the

57 Some conditions may be placed – for example, the national, if convicted, must be returned to his or her own country to serve the sentence.

traditional focus was on the service of summons. Nowadays, a wide range of measures are offered, such as in the area of asset recovery.

Mutual Recognition

The disappearance of national borders within the European Union has led to greater mobility and faster economic growth. Removing border checks, on the other hand, has also given a boost to cross-border crime.

With the rapidly advancing information technology, it is easier today, more than ever before, for a criminal to commit a serious crime in any given country without even being physically present. These reasons, as well as the terrorist attacks in the USA, Spain, and the UK, prompted EU member states to enhance mutual cooperation in criminal matters to ensure the safety and security of their citizens.

A simplified and accelerated procedure for procurement and transmission of evidence among EU member States would undoubtedly play a major role in fighting crimes with a cross-border element. In 1999, the EU has stressed that 'Mutual Recognition' shall become the cornerstone of judicial cooperation among the member States.[58]

The principle of Mutual Recognition in criminal matters means that a judicial decision issued by a competent authority in one member State will be directly recognized and enforced by a competent authority

58 Special EU Presidency Meeting was held in Tampere for the creation of an area of freedom, security, and justice in the EU.

in another member State. Therefore, judicial decisions are orders that have legal binding force upon the country receiving it.

European Arrest Warrant

In 2002, the European Arrest Warrant (EAW)[59] became the first instrument to embody the principle of mutual recognition in the field of criminal law. Since the introduction of EAW in July of 2002, the EU has smoothly extradited suspects of major crimes.

The EAW is an arrest warrant that allows the arrest of criminal suspects and their transfer for trial or detention which is valid throughout the EU. The EAW is an attempt to increase the speed of extradition throughout the EU. The EAW changes the mechanism from having a 'political and administrative phase' into a system operated directly through the judiciary.

The warrant is a judicial decision by a court of the member State for the arrest and subsequent surrender of a requested person in another member State. It is designed to meet the needs of justice, liberty, and security within a single region. The warrant can only be used for the purposes of conducting a criminal prosecution, carrying out a custodial sentence or a detention order. They only apply to criminal acts which have a maximum penalty of twelve months or more. Where a sentence has already been rendered, an EAW is also applicable to prison terms that are four months or longer.

---

59 www.europa.eu [European-arrest-warrant]

European Evidence Warrant

The European Evidence Warrant (EEW)[60] replaces the system of mutual assistance in criminal matters between member States for obtaining objects, documents, and data for use in criminal proceedings. Based on the framework decision of December 2008, EEW is a judicial decision which is issued by competent authorities designated by the member States.

An issuing authority may be a judge, court, investigating magistrate, public prosecutor or other judicial authority. Member States must also designate the competent authorities for recognizing and executing the EEW.

When the competent authority of an issuing State has reasonable grounds to believe that relevant evidence is located on the territory of another member State, it may transmit the EEW to the competent authority of that State. The EEW must be transmitted directly from the issuing authority to the executing authority and in a manner that leaves a written record.

To this end, member States may designate one or more central authorities that will assist the competent authorities. Member States may also take advantage of the secure telecommunications system of the European Judicial Network for the transmission of EEWs.

The EEW is to be recognized by the executing authority without any further formality. The executing authority shall take the necessary measures to execute the EEW, unless it decides to invoke a ground for

60 www.europa.eu [European-evidence-warrant]

non-recognition, non-execution or postponement.

Informal Cooperation

Prosecutors and law enforcement agents often resort to MLA without considering whether they should request formally for their need. Informal cooperation could be accomplished based on good faith and close relations of agencies. Sometimes, the country might even welcome an informal request that can be dealt with efficiently and expeditiously, depending on the nature of the cases.

The extent to which each country intends to assist without a formal request varies greatly. The willingness to assist depends on the relationship and current situation between the two States. In this context, the importance of building and maintaining close relations and friendship between law enforcement agencies in working level cannot be overemphasized.

The scope for informal cooperation cannot definitely be figured out. However, the tendency of informal cooperation can be observed in general. Firstly, regarding the routine request which does not ask the requested State to investigate based on compulsory measures, informal cooperation can be proceeded easily. Secondly, public records, such as property registration documents and corporation registration records, could be obtained by way of informal cooperation. Lastly, even the testimony of a witness may be taken if he or she is willing to do so voluntarily.

Generally speaking, cooperation outside the formal channels is possible as long as there is no conflict in domestic and international law. Moreover, informal cooperation has been proved the quicker and more effective way for gathering information and evidence in the investigation stage. In the viewpoint of field agents, informal cooperation needs to be put to use more widely.[61]

61 As it can be seen in later section, a firm establishment of a channel for 'direct contact and speedy response' may be a viable option to meet this need. Direct and efficient communication between the central authorities will inevitably enhance informal cooperation in more areas.

III. TRANSNATIONAL CASES IN KOREA

1. International Cooperation Procedure in Korea

Basic Procedure of Investigation

In Korea, criminal investigation organizations are divided into two categories – prosecutors and judicial police officers. Prosecutors' primary duties are to investigate crimes, direct police officers, initiate and maintain prosecution, and supervise the execution of legal sentences.[62] All investigative agencies transfer cases to the prosecutor and the public prosecutor completes the investigation and decides the case disposition. The judicial police officer has authority to initiate and conduct investigations under the supervision of the public prosecutor.

Accordingly, prosecutors direct and supervise the criminal investigation of the judicial police officers and the police follow the prosecutor's directions. As supervisors, it is essential for prosecutors to abide by the rule of law and due process which requires the protection

---

62 Prosecutors also lead state and administrative litigations and guide the litigation process so that it proceeds smoothly.

of human rights during the investigation.

When a crime occurs, the judicial police officer usually initiates the investigation. In reality, a police officer investigates ordinary crimes and street crimes, such as theft, violence, or traffic-related crimes. The case is transferred to the prosecutors' office where a prosecutor can continue the investigation if necessary. He does this either by ordering the police to investigate further or by directly questioning suspects, interviewing witnesses, and examining documents and other evidence. In the case of serious offences and white-collar crimes,[63] the prosecutor may initiate the investigation *ex officio* or without prior investigation by the judicial police officer.

Cooperative Instruments

Until the 1970s, the Korean Prosecution Service mainly focused on domestic crimes, like the most of other countries. With the 1988 Seoul Olympics, however, a new shift toward counteracting transnational crimes began to rise. Thereafter, the Korean National Assembly[64] enacted the Extradition Act. As international travel became more common and the number of foreign visitors to Korea increased, legislation became necessary to allow the development of more permanent cooperative relationships with foreign countries through

---

63 Examples of such crimes include high-profile bribery cases involving politicians and high ranking public officials, large-scale economic offences, narcotics offences, environmental offences, organized crimes, tax evasions, or police misconduct.

64 National Assembly is the highest legislature in the Republic of Korea.

bilateral treaties.

The following are the three major avenues for cooperation in criminal matters in Korea: (1) bilateral treaties, (2) multilateral conventions with provisions on legal assistance and extradition, and (3) informal cooperation in individual cases with countries that have not concluded a treaty with Korea.

Korea has extensive extradition and mutual legal assistance treaties that cover a vast scope of countries. Korea has also enacted laws to implement these treaties and to provide extradition and MLA without a treaty on the basis of reciprocity. Extradition and MLA are the most widely used methods for cooperation in Korea.

Extradition

Legal Framework

All extraditions in Korea are principally governed by the 'Extradition Act' and various bilateral and multilateral treaties to which Korea is a party. Created in 1988, the Extradition Act was made to 'promote international cooperation in the repression of crimes.'[65] Korea has signed bilateral extradition treaties with approximately thirty countries.[66] Aside from bilateral treaties, Korea signed the UNCAC on December 10, 2003 and ratified it on March 27, 2008. Korea has also

65 Korean Extradition Act, Article 1.

66 Detailed list provided in Appendix Table A.

signed the UNTOC but has not yet ratified it.

Overall, Korean Extradition Act and treaties follow most of the standards, principles and limitations of the international society. Like many countries, Korean extradition law allows for extradition in the absence of a treaty on the basis of reciprocity.

Korean Extradition Act
Article 4 – Reciprocity Principle

Even though no extradition treaty is concluded, if it is guaranteed that any State requesting an extradition would comply with an extradition request of the Republic of Korea with respect to the same or similar kind of extraditable crime, this Act shall be applicable.

See Principle of Double Criminality

Double criminality is also required in Korea. Extraditable offences are crimes that are punishable by imprisonment for life or more than one year under the laws of Korea and the requesting State.

Korean Extradition Act
Article 6 – Extraditable Crimes

Extradition may be requested only in cases where an extraditable crime corresponds to capital punishment or imprisonment without prison labor for life or not less than one year under the Acts of the Republic of Korea and the requesting State.

See Principle of Specialty

The principle of specialty can also be found in Korean extradition law as a limitation on extradition, although it is not literally called 'specialty.'

Korean Extradition Act
Article 10 – Guarantee on Prohibition of Punishment for Crimes Other than Crimes for Which Extradition Is Admitted

If there is no guarantee from a requesting State that an extradited criminal will not be punished for crimes other than those permitted to be extradited, and he will not be extradited to a third country, the criminal will not be extradited...

We can also see another example in Korean extradition treaty with the United States:

Korea and the United States Extradition Treaty
Article 15 – Rule of Specialty

1. A person extradited under this Treaty may not be detained, tried, or punished in the Requesting State except for:
a. The offence for which extradition has been granted...
b. An offence committed after the extradition of the person...

Grounds for Refusal

Like the *UN Model Treaty on Extradition*, the Korean Extradition Act also has both mandatory and discretionary grounds for refusal. The grounds for refusal in the Extradition Act are not, however, identical to the *Model Treaty on Extradition*. Both have a mandatory exception for political offences. Other mandatory grounds for refusal in the Extradition Act are as follows:

Korean Extradition Act
Article 7 – Absolute Cause for Denial of Extradition

No criminal shall be extradited in cases falling under any of the following subparagraphs:

1. Where the prescription of indictment or sentence against an extraditable crime is completed under the Acts of the Republic of Korea or the requesting State;
2. Where a trial for an extraditable crime is pending in a court of the Republic of Korea, or the judgment has become final;
3. Where there is no proper reason to suspect that the criminal committed an extraditable crime…;
4. Where it is deemed that… the criminal might be punished or subject to other unfavorable dispositions for the reasons of race, religion, nationality, sex, political belief, or membership in a specific group.

These articles are comparable to the exceptions of lapse of time, insufficient proof, pending prosecution and prejudice in the *Model Treaty*. These limitations can also be similarly incorporated in extradition treaties. For example, we can see the same or similar limitations in the extradition treaty between Korea and the U.S.:

Korea and U.S. Extradition Treaty
Article 4 – Political Offence

1. … Extradition shall not be granted if the Requested State determines that the offence for which extradition is requested is a political offence…

3. Surrender shall not be granted if…
   (a) The request… was in fact made for the primary purpose of prosecution or punishing the person sought on account of his race, religion, nationality or political opinion; or
   (b) Extradition has been requested for political purposes.

Korea and U.S. Extradition Treaty
Article 6 – Lapse of Time

Extradition may be denied… when prosecution or the punishment of the offence… would have been barred because of the statute of limitations…

Korea and U.S. Extradition Treaty
Article 7 – Prior Prosecution

Extradition shall not be granted when the person sought has been convicted or acquitted in the Requested State for the offence for which extradition is requested.

While negotiating the extradition treaty, the U.S. wanted to extend the scope of 'political offence' because they did not trust the political and criminal justice system of Korea at that time. The U.S. was worried that there would be many extradition requests from Korea to the U.S. mainly for political purposes. Finally, Korea agreed to stipulate the 'political purposes' clause in 3(b). Such a request, however, has never been made or denied.

There was the case in which extradition from Vietnam was denied on the ground of political offence:[67]

> Defendant N, a Vietnamese-American, was the founder and former Prime Minister of an anti-communist organization known as The Government of Free Vietnam (GFVN). He was detained by the Korean police in Seoul, Korea because the communist Vietnamese Government had accused the defendant of involvement in failed attempts to bomb its embassy in Thailand and state facilities in Vietnam (Possible charges of arms trafficking and acts of terrorism). After deliberation on July 27, 2006, the Seoul High Court rejected the Vietnamese request for extradition of the

67 This is the first, and by far the only case in which an extradition request was rejected by the Korean Court. It was a key case in which the traditional principle of non-extradition of political offenders collided with the recent trend of excluding terrorists from this principle. There has been a long-standing debate on whether this ruling had been appropriate.

defendant on the grounds of political offence exception.

Korean law also has grounds for discretionary denial. These are comparable to the optional exceptions of nationals, extraterritorial and humanitarian considerations in the *Model Treaty*.

Korean Extradition Act
Article 9 – Causes for Denial of Discretionary Extradition

No criminal may be extradited in the following cases:
1. Where the criminal is a citizen of the Republic of Korea
2. Where the whole or part of an extraditable crime has been committed in the territory of the Republic of Korea
3. Where a trial on a crime other than an extraditable crime ... is pending in the court of the Republic of Korea
4. Where the criminal was brought to trial and punished in the third country...
5. Where it is deemed inhuman to extradite a criminal in the light of the nature of the crime and the circumstances of the criminal

Procedure

Extradition requests are received by the Ministry of Foreign Affairs through diplomatic channels and transferred to the Ministry of Justice, which is the central authority for international cooperation in Korea. The Justice Ministry determines whether the request complies with an applicable treaty and whether it is reasonable to extradite the person requested.

The Minister of Justice can deny the request or make a review order of the request. If the request is denied, the Ministry of Justice notifies the fact to the Ministry of Foreign Affairs. With the extradition review order, the Ministry of Justice forwards the case to the Seoul

High Prosecutors' Office, which has exclusive jurisdiction over extraditions.

A prosecutor in the Seoul High Prosecutors' Office would initiate a court review of the extradition without delay, except in cases where it is not known where the criminal is. The prosecutor can request an extradition arrest warrant from the Seoul High Court unless the criminal is already in custody, or if the criminal has a consistent place of residence and there is no apprehension that the criminal might escape.[68]

In urgent cases, a foreign State may seek the provisional arrest of a person sought under the Extradition Act. The Act requires that a written request be sent via diplomatic channels, although bilateral treaties usually allow transmission without using such channels.

The Seoul High Court will proceed with the extradition review hearing without delay. Once the person is arrested, the prosecutor must seek an extradition review within three days. The Court determines whether the extradition is lawful and feasible. The Court can dismiss, deny, or permit the extradition.[69]

Even if the Court finds in favor of extradition, the Minister of Justice would further consider whether surrender could be refused in order to protect the interests of Korea.[70] If the Minister renders an extradition order, the prosecutor would surrender a criminal, who must be extradited

---

68 Korean Extradition Act, Article 19.

69 A request is rejected or dismissed if the request for extradition review is unlawful or is cancelled. A request is denied if it is deemed impossible to extradite the criminal. *See* Korean Extradition Act, Article 15(1).

70 Korean Extradition Act, Article 34.

within thirty days from the date of the decision, at the detention center to the public officer dispatched from the requested State.

As for requests for extradition to foreign States, the Minister of Justice has the sole authority. Requests must be sent via diplomatic channels except in urgent cases or if an applicable treaty provides otherwise. In case that the location of the person sought has been identified and his charge has been proved, the prosecutor in charge of the investigation will prepare and submit a written request for criminal

Process of Granting Extradition Request

1. Ministry of Foreign Affairs

- Receiving the request of extradition

2. Ministry of Justice

- Extradition review order
- Denial of request

3. Seoul High Prosecutors' Office

- Exclusive jurisdiction
- Initiate the court review
- Arrest criminal (extradition arrest warrant)

4. Seoul High Court

- Extradition review hearing
- Dismissal, denial, or permission of extradition

5. Ministry of Justice

- Extradition order
- Surrender criminal at detention center

extradition to the Ministry of Justice, via the Supreme Prosecutors' Office.

Statistics

A table detailing extradition statistics to and from Korea for the past two decades is provided in Appendix Table B. Escapes to the United States account for approximately forty percent of criminal escapees. Other major destinations for escapees include China, Australia, and the Philippines. Although not reflected in the table, financial crimes, such as fraud, embezzlement, and violation of the Illegal Check Control Act, comprise a majority of extradition cases.

Overall, while extraditions have greatly increased over the past decade, the fact that every year the number of accused offenders extradited to Korea surpasses the number extradited from Korea remains unchanged.

Mutual Legal Assistance

Legal Framework

The basis of MLA in Korea is the 'Act on International Judicial Mutual Assistance in Criminal Matters.' Enacted in 1991, Korean Act set out to promote international cooperation for the repression and prevention of crimes. The Act provides the scope and procedure of mutual assistance in requesting or responding to the request of any foreign country in connection with any investigation or trial of a criminal case.[71]

Various Mutual Legal Assistance Treaties (MLAT) to which Korea is a party also compose the legal framework for mutual legal assistance in Korea. Thus far, Korea has concluded Mutual Legal Assistance Treaties with 27 countries, and 25 of those treaties have been put into effect. As for countries with which treaties have not been concluded, the rule of reciprocity still enables legal assistance.[72] A full list of countries that have signed an MLA Treaty with Korea is provided in Appendix Table C.

One important aspect to note is that if a treaty is inconsistent with Korean Act, the provisions of the treaty shall prevail over the provisions of the Act.[73]

The scope of legal assistance provided in Korean Act is quite broad. It includes;

- taking the testimony or statement of persons for trial or investigation,
- providing documents, records, and articles of evidence,
- serving documents such as summons or subpoena,
- locating or identifying persons,
- transferring persons in custody for testimony, and

71 Korean Act on International Judicial Mutual Assistance in Criminal Matters, Article 1 (Purpose).

72 *Id.* Article 4 (Reciprocity) – Even in a case where a mutual assistance treaty has not been concluded, if there is a guarantee of a requesting country to comply with any request of the Republic of Korea for mutual assistance with respect to the same or similar matters, this Act shall be applicable.

73 *Id.* Article 3 (Relation with Mutual Assistance Treaty).

- executing requests for search and seizure.

Korean Act on International Judicial Mutual Assistance in Criminal Matters
Article 5 – Scope of Mutual Assistance

The scope of mutual assistance shall be as follows:
1. Investigation on where a person or object is;
2. Presentation of documents and records;
3. Service of documents, etc.;
4. Gathering of evidence, seizure, search, and verification;
5. Delivery of objects, such as evidence, etc.; and
6. Hearing of statements, and other measures to make any person testify or cooperate with the investigation in the requesting country.

Many of the standard principles and limitations that were explained earlier in the field of extradition are similarly displayed in the application of mutual legal assistance.

First of all, dual criminality is a discretionary limitation for MLA unless an applicable treaty provides otherwise. Korean Act does not prescribe evidentiary thresholds for rendering assistance, but an applicable treaty may do so, as provided in the MLAT between Korea and the U.S.

MLA Treaty between Korea and the United States
Article 3 – Limitations on Assistance

1. The Central Authority of the Requested State may deny assistance if ...
   d. ... the conduct which is the subject of the investigation, prosecution, or proceeding in the Requesting State would not constitute an offence under the laws of the Requested State.

With regards to the principle of specialty, Korean Act states the following:

Korean Act on International Judicial Mutual Assistance in Criminal Matters
Article 9 – Cooperation in Requesting Country

(2) ..., it shall be guaranteed by the requesting country that the party to such request for cooperation be exempted from any indictment or punishment, and any restriction on freedom, in the requesting country, for any act committed before.

The principle of specialty is more specifically worded in the MLA Treaty between Korea and the U.S.

MLA Treaty between Korea and the United States

Article 7 – Limitations on Use
The Requesting State shall not use any information or evidence obtained under this Treaty in any investigation, prosecution, or proceeding other than described in the request without the prior consent of the Requested State...
Article 12 – Safe Conduct
A person present in the Requesting State... shall not be subject to service of process, or be detained, prosecuted or subjected to any restriction of personal liberty by reason of acts or convictions which preceded that person's departure from the Requested State.

Restrictions

Korea may limit its assistance in the following ways, as depicted in Korean Act.[74] There are three main causes of limitation on MLA – political offence, human rights considerations, and essential state interests. They can be found in Article 3 of the MLAT between Korea

74 Many of the limitations were discussed in Section I, Chapter 3 (Grounds for Refusal).

and the U.S.

MLA Treaty between Korea and the United States
Article 3 – Limitations on Assistance

1. The Central Authority of the Requested State may deny assistance if ...
   a. the request relates to a political offence…;
   b. there are substantial grounds… to believe that compliance would facilitate the prosecution or punishment of the person to whom the request refers on account of his race, religion, nationality, or political opinions; and
   c. the execution of the request would prejudice the security or similar essential interests of the Requested States.

Korean Act on Judicial Mutual Assistance in Criminal Matters
Article 6 – Restriction on Mutual Assistance

It may not be required to give any mutual assistance, in a case which falls under any of the following subparagraphs:

1. Where it might be detrimental to the sovereignty, national security, public peace and order, or public morals, of the Republic of Korea;
2. Where it is deemed that the criminal might be punished, or subject to an unfavorable penal disposition, due to the race, nationality, sex, religion, social status, or the fact that he is a member of a specified social organization, or by the reason that he has a different political view;
3. Where it is deemed that the crime under mutual assistance is one of political nature, or the request for mutual assistance is made for the purpose of an investigation or trial on another crime of a political nature;
4. Where the crime under mutual assistance does not constitute a crime, or it is a crime against which no public action may be instituted, under the Act of the Republic of Korea; and
5. Where this Act prescribes that the requesting country should give a guarantee, but the requesting country fails to comply with it.

Procedure

Korean Act requires all incoming MLA requests, in writing, to be transmitted through diplomatic channels, except in urgent cases or if an applicable treaty provides otherwise.

In Korea, the central authority is the Ministry of Justice. Upon receiving an incoming request, the Ministry of Justice determines whether it is 'reasonable to comply with the request.' If so, the Ministry forwards the request to the appropriate agency for execution.

If the request is related to investigation, the Ministry of Justice sends it to the Prosecutor General, who forwards it to the District prosecutors' office. The following provisions from Korean Act on Judicial Mutual Assistance explain the procedure concerning Mutual Assistance Pertaining to Investigation at Request of Foreign Country:

Korean Act on International Judicial Mutual Assistance in Criminal Matters
Chapter III – Mutual Assistance Pertaining to Investigation at Request of Foreign Country

Article 11 (Acceptance of Request for, and Sending of Materials of, Mutual Assistance)

The acceptance of a request for mutual assistance, and the sending of materials of mutual assistance to the requesting country shall be made by the Minister of Foreign Affairs: If there are any urgent or special circumstances, the Minister of Justice may do it with the consent of the Minister of Foreign Affairs.

Article 14 (Action taken by Minister of Foreign Affairs)

The Minister of Foreign Affairs shall, upon receiving a request for mutual assistance pertaining to an investigation of a criminal case from a requesting country, send the written request for mutual assistance to the Minister of Justice together with related materials and his opinion.

Article 15 (Action taken by Minister of Justice)

… If the Minister of Justice deems after receiving the written request for mutual assistance, that it is reasonable to comply with the request, he shall … send related materials to the director of the district public prosecutors' office deemed necessary for mutual assistance, and … order him to take any measure necessary for mutual assistance …

If the request is related to a trial in court, the Ministry of Justice sends it to the Ministry of Administration in the Supreme Court. As to the procedure for providing mutual assistance with regards to criminal trial, Korean Act on Judicial Mutual Assistance states the following:

Korean Act on International Judicial Mutual Assistance in Criminal Matters
Chapter IV – Mutual Assistance as to Criminal Trial by Request of Foreign Country

Article 23 (Action Taken by Minister of Justice)
When the Minister of Justice receives a written request for mutual assistance as to a criminal trial to be administered by the court, he shall send it to the Ministry of Administration, Supreme Court.

Article 24 (Action Taken by Ministry of Administration, Supreme Court)
When the Ministry of Administration, Supreme Court receives a written request for mutual assistance as provided in Article 23 from the Minister of Justice, it shall send it to the president of a competent district court.

Cooperation may be also available at the law enforcement level besides formal MLA channels. The Korean Act on Judicial Mutual Assistance authorizes the Ministry of Public Administration and Security to seek and provide cooperation via Interpol. Available assistance includes exchange of information, identification of suspects, and investigative procedures that fall outside the formal MLA process.[75]

---

75 Korean Act on Judicial Mutual Assistance in Criminal Matters, Article 38 (Cooperation with International Criminal Police Organization).

Process for Mutual Assistance at the Request of a Foreign Country

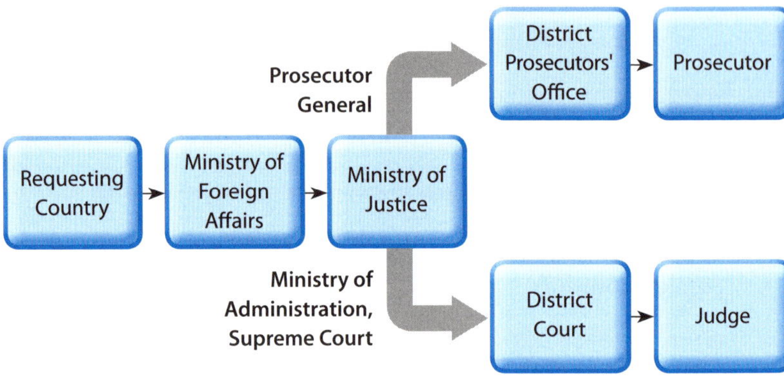

The results of the request are returned via the same route, but in reverse order.

Statistics

Recent statistics of MLA requests to and from Korea are provided in Appendix Table D-1 and Table D-2.

Transfer of Sentenced Persons

Legal Framework

The basis for the transferring of sentenced persons is the Korean Act on the International Transfer of Sentenced Persons.

Korean Act on the International Transfer of Sentenced Persons Article 1 – Purpose

Regarding a Korean National, or the like, who has been in prison after being sentenced in the final adjudication of an imprisonment penalty in a foreign country and a foreign national, who has been in prison after being sentenced in the final adjudication of an imprisonment in Korea, the Act stipulates the requirements and procedures necessary for the transfer of sentenced persons in order to promote rehabilitation and their smoother social integration.

Unlike extradition or mutual legal assistance, a prisoner's transfer is only possible between countries that have concluded treaties or agreements, and the rule of dual criminality may be applied.

Korea has been a party to the Council of Europe's Convention on Transfer of Sentenced Persons from November 1, 2005. With this membership, transfer of sentenced persons is now possible with 64 member countries without having to sign a separate treaty. In addition, Korea has signed bilateral treaties regarding the transfer of sentenced persons with five countries and is currently working on expanding that number to include Vietnam, the Philippines, Thailand, Peru and Qatar. A table detailing these treaties is provided in Appendix Table E.

Recently, demand for using this mechanism is expected to increase. As of 2012, in Korea, there are approximately 1,200 foreigners who have been sentenced and are in need of transferring. On the other hand, about 1,600 Korean nationals have been sentenced in foreign countries.

Procedure

In Korea, when there is a request for transferring the sentenced

Actual Example of a Request for Transfer

U.S. Department of Justice

10th & Constitution Avenue, N.W.
Criminal Division
Office of Enforcement Operations

International Prisoner Transfer Unit
John C. Keeney Building, 12th Floor
Washington, D.C. 20530

000
Director Prosecutor
International Criminal Affairs Division
Ministry of Justice
Government Complex Gwacheon
427-720, Republic of Korea

Re: XXX , Prisoner Number
Approval of Request to Transfer to the United States Under the
Convention on the Transfer of Sentenced Persons

Dear 000

The United States has approved the request of the above-referenced American national to be transferred to the United States pursuant to the Council of Europe Convention on the Transfer of Sentenced Persons to serve the balance of his sentence imposed by a court in Korea.

In accordance with Article 6.1 of the Convention, please find the following attachments:

1. Confirmation that the prisoner is a United States national for the purposes of the Convention (Attachment A);

2. Statement as to dual criminality and a copy of the relevant law which provides that the offense for which he is in custody in Korea would constitute a criminal offense if committed in the United States (Attachment B);

3. A statement that the "continued enforcement" provision of the Convention would be applied (Attachment C).

In addition, we have attached two copies of an explanation of the procedures for determining a release date in the United States (Attachment D).

person, the Ministry of Justice as a central authority will take the initiative and make the final decision after consultation with the Prosecution Service and the Ministry of Foreign Affairs. The severity of the crime, rehabilitation of the victim, attitude of the inmate, and other factors will be given consideration in the process. For example, if the inmate is imprisoned due to financial or property crimes, damage compensation is an important factor in deciding whether to transfer the prisoner.

Process for the Transfer of Sentenced Persons *from Korea to Abroad*

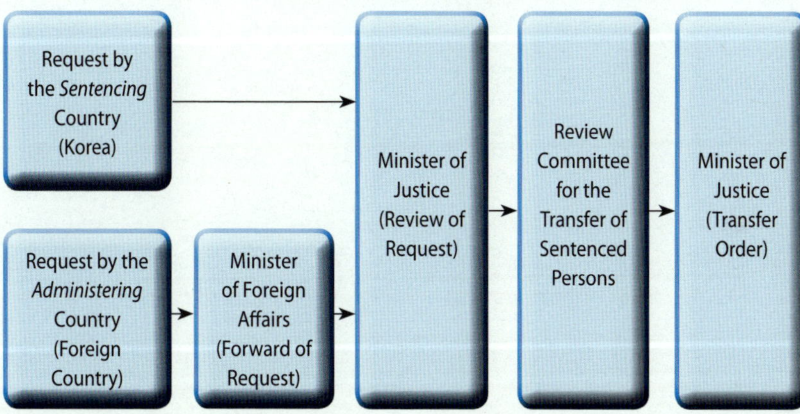

Statistics

Recent statistics for prisoner transfer requests to and from Korea are provided in Appendix Chart F-1 and F-2, respectively.

2. English Instructor Murder Case

Summary of the Case

Defendant *KP* committed murder against her co-worker in Korea. Both were American citizens. As *KP* fled to the U.S. after the crime, Korea requested to the U.S. the extradition of *KP*. However, the U.S. rejected the request because there was no extradition treaty between the two countries. Later, mutual legal assistance was requested by the U.S. However, Korea was unable to assist due to the official destruction of evidence. This case is a classic example of how failed efforts in both extradition and legal assistance can lead to an unfortunate outcome of the defendant escaping from punishment.

Defendant Fled to the U.S. after Committing Murder in Korea

The victim was a co-worker of the defendant *KP* at English Institute in Seoul, South Korea. On December 20, 1988, *KP* walked into the victim's residence and repeatedly stabbed the victim with a kitchen knife. The victim died on the scene.

Regarding the murder of the victim, an accomplice was prosecuted for aiding *KP*'s escape from Korea and for eliminating evidence from the crime scene. The accomplice was a co-worker of *KP* at the English Institute and also *KP*'s roommate. As *KP* felt constant pressure from the police investigation, the accomplice advised her to flee the country and go back home in the U.S. Also, the accomplice stated during the police investigation that *KP* had not killed the victim despite having heard *KP*'s confession. This false report during investigations from December 20, 1988 to February 27, 1989 led the police to believe *KP*'s alibi and *KP* was able to flee Korea on January 15, 1989.

Upon her departure, the Korean police began to focus their attention on *KP* as the main suspect for the murder. Even though successful investigation led to the prosecution of the accomplice on charges of eliminating evidence and providing aid to the criminal, justice seems unfulfilled as *KP* had fled to the U.S. without any prosecution.

On September 27, 1989, the Korean government made a request to the U.S. for the extradition of *KP* in order to clarify the truth and preserve the balance of punishment between *KP* and the accomplice.

But the United States denied the request on the ground that there was no extradition treaty at the time of the request.[76] The U.S. had sustained a 'No Treaty, No Extradition' policy. Furthermore, *KP* was a

76 The Extradition Treaty between Korea and the U.S. was signed in 1998 and entered into force in 1999.

citizen of the U.S.

In addition, the U.S. decided that it had no jurisdiction over the case because the U.S. bases its jurisdiction on the principle of territoriality,[77] which only allows jurisdiction over conduct that takes place within the territory of a state. Since the murder had taken place in a foreign country, the U.S. did not have jurisdiction over this case.

To solve this matter, the family of the victim asked the U.S. to punish *KP* and brought a civil claim of wrongful death against her. When *KP* testified as a witness saying, "I did not kill her," the U.S. indicted *KP* on charges of perjury. However, this was not successful and as a result, neither Korea nor the United States could hold *KP* accountable for her criminal act.

5 Years Later..
Case Entered a New Phase; New Enactment

What seemed like an unfortunate ending to the case entered a different phase on March 1, 1994 when the U.S. wrote a letter to discuss 'the potential prosecution in the United States of the Defendant *KP*' to the Korean Embassy in the U.S.[78]

---

77 The principle of territoriality allows for jurisdiction over conduct that takes place within the territorial boundaries of the state. The principle of nationality bases jurisdiction on the allegiance or nationality of the perpetrator of the offences as prescribed by the state of his allegiance, no matter where the offences take place.

78 Five years later, when the author of this book was working in the Korean embassy in the U.S., the author received an official letter from his counterpart in the U.S. Department Of Justice on March 1, 1994. The letter discussed the "potential prosecution of the Defendant in the United States ."

Letter to the Legal Attaché in the Korean Embassy, March 1, 1994

U. S. Department of Justice

Criminal Division

Washington, D.C. 20530

March 1, 1994

Kim, Joon-Gyu
Legal Attache
Korean Embassy
2450 Massachusetts Avenue, N.W.
Washington, D.C. 20008

Subject: Potential prosecution in the United States of
P .

Dear Mr. Kim:

As you know, in the Fall of 1994, Congress enacted a new provision, Section 1119 of Title 18 of the Untied States Code, making punishable the murder outside of the United States of one U.S. citizen by another U.S. citizen. As a result of the enactment of that law, the United States is currently investigating whether P murdered in Korea in 1988.

I have today received a letter from the United States Attorney for the Western District of Washington, a copy of which is attached, seeking a list of the evidence in the above case presently in the possession of Korean authorities. I respectfully request that you obtain such a list and forward it to me as soon as possible. Once the United States government has received and reviewed the list, I will contact you to discuss the possibility of and procedure for U.S. authorities to have some or all of the evidence scientifically tested as part of the U.S. investigation.

If you have any further questions, please do not hesitate to call me at (202) 514-0036. I look forward to your response.

Sincerely,

George W. Proctor
Director
Office of International Affairs
Criminal Division

by:

Kenneth J. Harris
Senior Trial Attorney

The U.S. Congress had enacted a new provision, Section 1119 of Title 18 of the United States Code,[79] that states, "a person who, being a national of the United States, kills or attempts to kill a national of the United States while such national is outside the United States but within the jurisdiction of another country shall be punished as provided under sections 1111, 1112, and 1113." As a result, the U.S. had begun to reinvestigate whether *KP* had murdered the victim in Korea in 1988.

§1119. Foreign murder of United States nationals

(a) Definition – In this section, 'national of the United States' has the meaning stated in section 101(a)(22) of the Immigration and Nationality Act (8 U.S.C. 1101(a)(22)).

(b) Offence – A person who, being a national of the United States, kills or attempts to kill a national of the United States while such national is outside the United States but within the jurisdiction of another country shall be punished as provided under sections 1111, 1112, and 1113.

Matters of Jurisdiction

The efforts displayed by the U.S. Congress to make a new enactment should be recognized. Whereas most States neglect taking further steps to pursue a criminal, it was different in that legal grounds were secured to prevent such an unfortunate case from happening again.

---

79 It is noteworthy that this legislation was first brought up by the North Carolina Congressman who represented the state where the victim was from. In efforts to prevent unfortunate outcomes such as that of the victim, the Congressman made initial efforts to pass *The Crime Bill of 1994*. Subsequently, it was discussed during the 103rd Congress and it resulted in the enactment of *The Violent Crime Control and Law Enforcement Act of 1994*.

Letter from the Assistant U.S. Attorney, January 23, 1995.

UNITED STATES ATTORNEY
Western District of Washington
800 Fifth Avenue, Suite 3600
Seattle, Washington 98104-3190

TEL (206) 553-7970
FAX (206) 553-0882

Please reply to:
Robert G. Chadwell
Assistant United States Attorney
Direct line: (206) 553-4734

January 23, 1995

Mr. Kenneth Harris
United States Department of Justice
Office of International Affairs
Criminal Investigation Division
P.O. Box 27330
Washington, DC 20036

Re: <u>United States v. KP</u>
USAO 8901179

Dear Mr. Harris:

I have completed my factual review and reinvestigation of the murder of victim which occurred in Korea on December 20, 1988. This reinvestigation included a reexamination of all files in the custody of the F.B.I., Army CID, and the United States Attorneys Office as well as reinterviews of the major witnesses, including Taimi Ames Metzler. In my professional opinion, the evidence presently available is insufficient to charge and convict Kathy Patrick.

Any prosecution of KP must rely on the testimony of her then roommate, Taimi Ames (now Metzler). Ms. Metzler would testify that she was awakened at approximately 2:00 a.m. on December 20, 1988 by KP . Ms. P told M that she had just killed victim with knife. Ms. M accompanied P back to the apartment where victim was found dead. Ms. Abel's throat had been cut and she had been stabbed several times.

Unfortunately, roommate did not tell authorities about Ms. Patrick's involvement until about two months after the murder and well after KP had left Korea. Ms. M attributes hr failure to come forward to "repressed memory", something brought about by the mind attempting to suppress memories of a particularly shocking event. Equally troubling are the multiple statements given by Ms. M to Army CID investigators in Korea during her attempts to retrieve her "repressed memories." In one of these statements, which recanted shortly after giving it, she admitted to committing the murder itself. (However, her version does not fit with the physical evidence.)

Ms. M initial statement is consistent with the physical evidence and the medical evidence contained in the autopsy. Furthermore, it provides a reasonable and believable motive for Ms. KP to have committed the murder. Much of the motive evidence can be corroborated and there is independent evidence of prior assaultive behavior by Ms. KP . The weakness in our case is the lack of corroborative evidence that KP actually committed the murder.

There is some chance that such evidence exists and is in the custody of the Korean National Police. Ms. A died after a violent and bloody struggle with her attacker. Because of the nature of the defensive wounds on Ms. A 's hand there is the strong possibility that she scratched her killer during the attack. According to the medical reports, fingernail scrapings were taken from Ms. A .

There is also evidence that the killer was injured to some degree in the attack. Band aid wrappers were found on the floor inside the A apartment near the front door, indicating that the killer required at least minimal first aid. The attacker also attempted to clean up the apartment as indicated by the condition of the bathroom and the towel which was placed over the victim's hands. Ms. M recalls P showing her a scrape or scratch on the leg. KP told M that " had done this."

The police reports and photographs depict blood on the floor a short distance from the bed where the victim was found. Because the overwhelming majority of blood was limited to the victim's bed, it appears likely that Ms. A was attacked while she lay in the bed and remained there through the struggle to her death. Police reports indicate that numerous bloodstains were observed and presumably samples taken.

Members of an Army lab team examined the murder scene about a month after the murder and collected some blood samples and hair samples. After preliminary testing, the samples were returned to the Korean National Police.

I am told by forensic experts that DNA testing is possible despite the passage of time. At this point, such testing appears to be the only avenue of obtaining the type on strong evidence needed to go forward. Our telephone conversations have raised a question about what items of evidence are still in the custody of the Korean National Police or the Ministry of Justice. I am ready and willing to travel to Korea if visble evidence is still in existence, but believe that questions as to the status of evidence should be answered first.

It is important to learn if any of the following items of evidence still exist and, if so, where are they presently held?

1. The knife used to kill victim
2. Fingernail scrapings taken from KP
3. Sample of blood taken from Ms. Abel during the autopsy
4. Samples of blood taken from the murder scene, including bloody bedclothing, items of clothing, etc.
5. Band Aid wrappers
6. Hair samples
7. Items seized from Kaimi Ames or her apartment which might contain blood stains

If other items which potentially contain the bodily fluids of the killer are also being held, those items could prove important as well.

Please pass my inquiries along to the appropriate members of the Korea diplomatic staff in Washington, D.C. and give them my thanks for their assistance.

Sincerely,

KATRINA C. PFLAUMER
United States Attorney

ROBERT G. CHADWELL
Assistant United States Attorney

With the possibility of punishing a U.S. national who kills or attempts to kill another U.S. national in a jurisdiction outside of the U.S., it can be interpreted as meaning that jurisdiction has been stretched to encompass boundaries beyond the U.S. With such measures to extend the limits posed by jurisdiction issues, it has now become possible to administer justice in the harshest and most unfortunate circumstances.

The Director of the Office of International Affairs in the U.S. Department of Justice sent a letter on March 1, 1994[80] because the U.S. Attorney for the Western District of Washington, the state in which *KP* was residing, had initially sought a list of evidence for the *KP* case presently in the possession of Korean authorities.

Actual Evidence Needed for DNA Testing

The U.S. hoped to prove their case again *KP* through DNA testing. In furtherance of the case, the U.S. Attorney's Office of the Western District of Washington again sent a letter to the U.S. Department of Justice.

The letter states that "after factual review and reinvestigation of the murder of the victim, the evidence presently available is insufficient to charge and convict *KP*. The weakness in the case lays in the lack of corroborative evidence that *KP* actually committed the murder."

It also states that "as it has been told by forensic experts that

80 The letter is on the previous page (p. 88).

DNA testing is possible despite the passage of time, at this point, such testing appears to be the only avenue of obtaining the type on strong evidence needed to go forward." The letter ends by noting that "it is important to learn if any of the following items of evidence still exist and, if so, where are they presently held?

1. The knife used to kill the victim
2. Fingernail scrapings taken from the victim or *KP*
3. Sample of blood taken from the victim during the autopsy
4. Samples of blood taken from the murder scene, including bloody bed-clothing, items of clothing, etc.
5. Band aid wrappers
6. Hair samples
7. Items seized from the accomplice or her apartment which might contain blood stains." [81]

Destruction of Evidence

However, the physical evidences had been officially destroyed after the period of evidence-preservation had ended. The Korean prosecutors' office had closed the case. There seemed to be no possibility of having *KP* extradited or prosecuted in the U.S. Critical evidence such as fingernail scrapings and other evidence that would lead to a possible DNA testing had been destroyed before the request

81 Letter from the Assistant U.S. Attorney, January 23, 1995.

from the U.S.[82]

After contacting the responsible prosecutor in Korea, the legal attaché of the Korean Embassy replied back with the unfortunate news. He stated,

"It is very regrettable to inform you that all the material evidence of the KP case was officially destroyed on April 27, 1993. The Eastern Branch Office of the Seoul District Public Prosecutors' Office had made an investigation of the murder case and kept the evidence until the date of official destruction. Officials decided to abandon the evidence of this case since there seemed to be no possibility to extradite or have a court trial in the U.S." [83]

As the relevant law that made punishable the murder of one U.S. citizen by another U.S. citizen outside of the U.S. was enacted in the fall of 1994, it was unfortunate that the evidence had been destroyed far before such measures were made. As a result, the possibility of punishing *KP* in the U.S. by way of applying the new law was eliminated. It was regrettable that Korea and the U.S. had no informal correspondence regarding the new enactment process and the possible punishment of *KP* before the official destruction of the evidence.[84]

82 Not because of the statute of limitation, but because of the administrative time limit for the preservation of evidence in the prosecutors' office.

83 Letter from the Legal Attaché in Korean Emassy, February 24, 1995.

84 It is worth noting that direct and closer cooperation between law enforcement agents worldwide is necessary to bring justice even to simple murder case like this one.

Letter from the Legal Attaché in Korean Embassy, February 24, 1995

EMBASSY OF THE REPUBLIC OF KOREA
WASHINGTON, D. C.

February 24, 1995

Mr. George W. Proctor
Director, Office of International Affairs
Criminal Division
U.S. Department of Justice

Dear Mr. Proctor,

I have received your fax in regard to the case about ____KP____ and have contacted the Ministry of Justice in Korea to respond to your inquiry about the use of the evidence in this case.

It is very regrettable to inform you that all the material evidence of the _KP_ case was officially destroyed on April 27, 1993. The Eastern Branch Office of the District Public Prosecutor's Office in Seoul had made an investigation of the _KP_ murder case and kept the evidence until the date of official destruction. Officials decided to abandon the evidence of this case since there seemed to be no possibility to extradite or have a court trial in the U.S.

The new provision of the U.S. Code, which enables to punish the murder outside the U.S. of one U.S. citizen by another U.S. citizen, was enacted in October of 1994. The Korean Prosecutor's Office had not been informed of the enactment of this new law and therefore was unable to pursue the possibility of punishing ____KP____ in the U.S. by way of applying the new law.

I am afraid that a DNA test, which the U.S. attorney in the Western District of Washington suggested to substantiate the evidence of the _KP_ case, will not be possible. However, I heard from the Ministry of Justice that the District Prosecutor's Office in Seoul has kept the investigation document and the report of the forensic analysis of the evidence.

If we can offer further assistance in proving the _KP_ murder case, the Korean Ministry of Justice and Prosecutor's Office are willing to cooperate with your office and the U.S. Attorney in the Western District of Washington. All the Korean prosecutors, including myself, hope to bring justice in the _KP_ murder case.

I look forward to seeing you soon again.

Sincerely,

Joon Gyu Kim
Legal Attache

Future Promises

On March 9, 1995, the Director of the Office of International Affairs within the U.S. Department of Justice wrote back to the Legal Attaché of the Korean Embassy.

He addressed the situation by stating that "I share your regret regarding the resulting inability of U.S. investigative agencies to conduct further scientific tests as part of our investigation into the murder of the victim. Although at present the United States will not seek an indictment in this case, our investigation remains open. Accordingly, I request that your authorities coordinate with us any significant future developments in this case."

It is stated in the letter that "If you foresee the possibility of seeking the return of *KP* to the Republic of Korea – should current extradition negotiations lead to the conclusion of an extradition treaty in the near future – we will be pleased to coordinate our investigative effort with you."

Although it is unfortunate to note that subsequent measures by both countries did not lead to the prosecution of *KP*, the extradition negotiations had successfully led to the conclusion of an extradition treaty between Korea and the U.S. in 1998. It entered into force on December 20, 1999. Also, it is worth noting that the *Treaty between the Republic of Korea and the United States of America on Mutual Legal Assistance in Criminal Matters* was signed (1993) and ratified (1997)

Letter to the Legal Attaché from OIA, March 9, 1995

U. S. Department of Justice

Washington, D.C. 20530

March 9, 1995

Kim, Joon-Gyu
Legal Attache
Embassy of Korea
2450 Mass. Avenue, N.W.
Washington, D.C. 20008

Dear Mr. Kim:

I am in receipt of your letter of February 24, 1995, advising of the destruction of physical evidence gathered by Korean authorities at the time of the 1988 murder of A . I share your regret regarding the resulting inability of U.S. investigative agencies to conduct further scientific tests as part of our investigation into the murder of A .

Although at present the United States will not seek an indictment in this case, our investigation remains open. Accordingly, I request that your authorities coordinate with us any significant future developments in this case. For example, should law enforcement authorities in the Republic of Korea obtain any further evidence related to this matter, we would be grateful if you would preserve the evidence and advise us of your actions. Additionally, if you foresee the possibility of seeking the return of P to the Republic of Korea -- should current extradition negotiations lead to the conclusion of an extradition treaty in the near future -- we will be pleased to coordinate our investigative effort with you.

Sincerely,

George W. Proctor
Director
Office of International Affairs
Criminal Division

by: Kenneth J. Harris
Senior Trial Attorney

as well.[85]

If the same case were to arise today, the outcome would be different. The Extradition Treaty between the U.S. and Korea has entered into force, and extradition from the U.S. is now possible. However, even if there is a treaty, the U.S. may not have extradited *KP* to Korea because she is a U.S. citizen.

Exemplary Case of Failure

English Instructor Murder Case presents us with an unfortunate lesson as the criminal walked away without any punishment in both Korea and the U.S. The two States were unable to cooperate on extraditing the criminal because there was no treaty between the two countries. Mutual legal assistance also failed due to the lack of informal contact between the two countries before the official abandonment of evidence.

This can be an exemplary case that shows how failed efforts in both extradition and mutual legal assistance can lead to an undesirable outcome where justice is not administered.

85 Thereafter, Korea did not make a request to the U.S. for the extradition of *KP*.

Case Timetable

Date	Event
1988. 12. 20	Murder between U.S. citizens occurred in Korea – Korean National Police Agency instigated investigation.
1989. 1. 15	*KP* fled to the U.S.
1989. 7. 12	Accomplice was prosecuted for 1) elimination of evidence; and 2) aiding the criminal.
1989. 9. 27	Korea made extradition request regarding *KP* to the U.S.
1989. 11. 28	U.S. denied the extradition request from Korea since no extradition treaty existed between the two countries as of this time.
1993. 4. 27	Korean officials abandoned evidence of this case since there seemed to be no possibility of extradition or a court trial in the U.S.
1994. 3. 1	U.S. requested evidence from Korea, based on the new enactment of Foreign Murder of United States Nationals.
1995. 2. 24	Korean Legal Attaché informed that all the material evidence had been destroyed. Therefore, no evidence was provided.
1998. 6. 9	Extradition Treaty between Korea and the U.S. was signed and entered into force on 1999. 12. 20.

3. Fled Rapist Case

Summary of the Case

Korean resident *JA* kidnapped and raped a Japanese female in New Jersey, U.S. While under investigation, *JA* fled to Korea upon release after posting bail. The U.S. requested extradition of *JA* to Korea. Despite the denial of such request by Korea due to a lack of an extradition treaty, mutual legal assistance between the two countries successfully led to the eventual punishment of *JA* in the Korean court.

JA Fled to Korea after Committing Rape

JA, 18 at the time of crime, was charged with the kidnapping and sexual assault of a 22-year-old woman. On July 31, 1993, *JA* and another suspect abducted the Japanese female from the parking lot of the victim's workplace. After being forced into her own vehicle, the victim was taken to a motel where she was repeatedly raped and sexually abused at gun point. *JA* and the accomplice had even called the victim's father and demanded that a ransom be paid for his daughter.

JA and his accomplice *Kim*, both Korean nationals, were arrested afterwards. *Kim* made a confession linking himself and *JA* to the crimes. Upon arrest, *Kim* and *JA* were held at the Bergen County Jail in Hackensack. However, *JA* was on a $350,000 cash bail and released after posting bail in cash. *JA*'s estranged father, a wealthy Korean businessman, apparently secured his son's release by posting his bail. Although *JA* was scheduled to appear in court on March 24, 1994, he jumped bail and fled to Korea.

Flow Chart of the Case Proceedings

JA, Indicted in New Jersey and Found in Korea

Following his jump on bail, an indictment was filed against *JA* on September 30, 1994, in the Superior Court of New Jersey, Bergen County. *JA* was charged with such offences as kidnapping, theft of a motor vehicle, aggravated sexual assault, aggravated criminal sexual contact, possession of a weapon and attempted extortion.

It took a long time for the Korean police and prosecutors to locate *JA* because they had little information and no evidence. Eventually, they found him in Seoul.

Article from *The Record*, local newspaper in North Jersey, Oct. 13, 1994

-10 THE RECORD FROM PAGE ONE

FUGITIVE: Accused rapist jumped bail

from Page A-1

Plaza in Edgewater and taken to a Fort Lee motel where she was repeatedly raped at gunpoint.

"We don't believe that in this case there was a safety problem for anybody, including the victim and her family. We believe he's not stayed in the metropolitan area," Fahy said.

Fahy said his office routinely withholds information about fugitives. "Our job is to catch the people, and it makes it easier to do," he said.

During an emotional interview Wednesday, Jang's mother, who asked that her name be withheld, said that although her son refused to reveal his whereabouts when he called her, she doubted that he fled to Korea because he and his father did not have a close relationship. She said she last spoke to Jang in May.

"I took him here [Leonia] when he was 6, I was a single parent then and took care of him. He only sees his natural father once a year," she said.

She also said that when she contacted her ex-husband he did not know his son's whereabouts and was angry because he had forfeited the $350,000 he put up for his son's release.

"If he would contact me now, I hope he will come back and face the case. After calling me three times to say he was OK, he never called again," she said. She cried

JA

Under a plea bargain that was to have been consummated in March with the Bergen County prosecutor's office, Jang would have had to serve years in jail, said Harvey Kaminsky, Jang's New York City attorney. Kaminsky said the actual number of years had not been negotiated yet.

Jang, who lived with his mother and stepfather in Leonia for 10 years, was expected to plead guilty to both kidnapping and sexual assault, he said.

JOHN J. FAHY
Concedes mistakes

That bail was set even though Jang had eluded authorities after the alleged crimes and was accused of plotting an armed breakout from the detention center days after arriving there.

Moses had the ability to increase the bail mainly because of Jang's alleged plot to escape and lack of citizenship. Assistant County Prosecutor Ike Gavzy, who handled the case as head of the sex crimes unit, also could have asked Moses that bail be raised, but did not.

"We don't believe that in this case there was a safety problem for anybody."

John J. Fahy
Bergen County prosecutor

Although he wasn't a very good student, he enjoyed sports and played tennis often, his mother said. As a youth, he played football but stopped when he was diagnosed as having high blood pressure, she said.

For Palisades Park resident Jason Kim and many of his friends in North Jersey's Korean community, the news that an alleged Korean rapist had jumped bail in Bergen County was no news at all. It had been on the community grapevine for months.

"It's pretty much common knowledge to people," said Kim, president of the Korean American Voters Association in Englewood. "In fact, we knew about it months ago."

Kim and others interviewed Wednesday said Jun Ho Jang was probably safely holed up in his native country or, at least, hiding out

Kin think alleged rapist was in area

But Fahy believes fugitive fled U.S.

By JIM CONSOLI
Staff Writer

Since jumping bail earlier this year, accused rapist Jang has contacted his family in Leonia at least three times, leading his mother to believe that he may have stayed with friends in the metropolitan area.

But Bergen County Prosecutor John J. Fahy said he believes Jang fled the country months ago, possibly to Korea, where his father lives.

Fahy repeated earlier statements that his office is working with the FBI's fugitive squad, Interpol, and Korean authorities to track down Jang. He would not comment specifically on whether authorities contacted Jang's estranged father, a wealthy Korean electronics mogul named Chang, who secured his son's release by posting $350,000 cash bail last year.

He also was unable to explain how Jang could have fled the country after surrendering his passport under a judge's order.

"We're actively pursuing Mr. Jang with a warrant for his arrest," Fahy said.

Fahy said his office chose not to reveal publicly that it had known since March that Jang had jumped bail, saying there was no risk to the community. Jang, 18, is charged with the kidnapping and sexual assault of a 22-year-old Palisades Park woman. Officials said the woman was abducted from the parking lot of

Letter from the Bergen County Prosecutor to the Korean Ambassador, Dec. 14, 1994

Office of the County Prosecutor

County of Bergen

HACKENSACK, NEW JERSEY 07601

(201) 646-2300

John J. Fahy
Prosecutor

Frank Puccio
First Assistant Prosecutor

Michael J. Tobin
Chief of Investigators

December 14, 1994

Ambassador Seung-Soo Han
Korean Ambassador
2450 Massachusetts Avenue, North West
Washington, DC 20008

Re: JA

Dear Ambassador Seung-Soo Han:

It has come to my attention that JA is currently residing at Seoul, Korea. This has been corroborated by Lt. Kim Tae Chol, the Republic of Korea Police liaison officer to the United States Embassy in Korea.

It is my understanding that JA'S immigration record shows that he is still in the United States and that he entered Korea with a false Korean passport.

I again request that he be sent back to the United States. The Bergen County Prosecutor's Office will pay all necessary expenses relative to the extradition, expulsion or deportation of JA.

Very truly yours,

JOHN J. FAHY
Bergen County Prosecutor

U.S. Made Extradition Request for *JA*

After locating *JA*, the initial action taken by the Bergen County Prosecutors' Office was to send the Congressman who represented the district to the Korean Embassy to seek assistance and ask that *JA* be sent back to the U.S. The Bergen County Prosecutors' Office was willing to pay all necessary expenses related to this process. However, this kind of political approach was of no use in solving the problem.[86]

Thereafter, the Office of International Affairs in the Department of Justice asked the Department of State to send a diplomatic note to the Embassy of the United States in Korea, which was transmitted to the Korean Government. The U.S. requested cooperation from Korean authorities for the expulsion, deportation, extradition, or alternative prosecution in Korea. This formal request letter on November 17, 1994 concerns: 'United States Request to the Republic of Korea for the Extradition, Deportation, or Expulsion of *JA* or, alternatively, Prosecution in Korea.'

After the formal request letter by the OIA,[87] subsequent actions

---

86 As for the legal approach, the Legal Attaché in the Korean Embassy advised the Bergen County prosecutor to try legal methods for cooperation, such as extradition.

87 The United States Attorney Manual (USAM) states the following:

The Office of International Affairs (OIA) provides information and advice to Federal and State prosecutors about the procedure for requesting extradition from abroad. OIA also advises and provides support to Federal prosecutors handling foreign extradition requests for fugitives found in the United States.

Every formal request for international extradition based on Federal criminal charges must be reviewed and approved by OIA. At the request of the Department of State, formal requests based on State charges are also reviewed by OIA before submission to the Department of State ...(USAM 9-15.210 Role of the Office of International Affairs)

Letter from the Department of Justice to the Department of State, November 17, 1994

U. S. Department of Justice
Criminal Division

Washington, D.C. 20530

GWP:LCB:KJH:LFC
95-100-8206

November 17, 1994

BY E-MAIL

Robert Harris, Esq.
Assistant Legal Adviser
Law Enforcement and Intelligence
Department of State
2201 C Street, N.W.
Room 5419-A
Washington, D.C. 20520-6310

Attn: Daphne Wilson or Michel Bassle

Dear Mr. Harris:

Re: United States Request to the Republic of Korea for the Extradition, Deportation, or Expulsion of __________, a/k/a "__________", or, Alternatively, Prosecution In Korea

The Office of International Affairs requests that the Department of State send a diplomatic note along the following lines to the Embassy of the United States in Korea, for transmission to the Government of Korea, with respect to the above-referenced request for expulsion, deportation, extradition, or local prosecution.

BEGIN TEXT

1. ORGIN:

This message is sent at the request of the Office of International Affairs, Criminal Division, U.S. Department of Justice, which coordinates all extraditions to and from the United States.

2. REQUEST FOR EXPULSION OR EXTRADITION:

At the request of the Office of the County Prosecutor, County of Bergen, Hackensack, New Jersey, the United States requests the

---

Procedures for requesting extradition from abroad are stated in the Criminal Resource Manual at 602:

Extradition involves four basic steps:

1) Contacting the Office of International Affairs;

2) Making a preliminary determination of extraditability;

3) Deciding whether to ask for provisional arrest; and

4) Submitting the required documents in support of the formal request for extradition.

Letter from Congressman to Korean Ambassador, December 1, 1994

ROBERT G. TORRICELLI
9TH DISTRICT, NEW JERSEY

COMMITTEES:
FOREIGN AFFAIRS
CHAIRMAN: SUBCOMMITTEE ON WESTERN HEMISPHERE AFFAIRS
SCIENCE, SPACE, AND TECHNOLOGY
SELECT INTELLIGENCE

Congress of the United States
House of Representatives
Washington, DC 20515-3009

WASHINGTON OFFICE:
2159 RAYBURN HOUSE OFFICE BUILDING
WASHINGTON, DC 20515-3009
202-225-5061

DISTRICT OFFICES:
COURT PLAZA
25 MAIN STREET
HACKENSACK, NJ 07601
201-646-1111

14A PATH PLAZA
JERSEY CITY, NJ 07306
201-222-6100

December 1, 1994

H.E. Seung-Soo Han
Ambassador
The Embassy of Korea
Washington, D.C.

Dear Mr. Ambassador:

I would like to request your assistance in bringing to justice Mr. JA , an 18 year-old Korean national and long-time resident of New Jersey.

As you know, Mr. JA is accused of kidnapping and raping a 22 year-old woman at gunpoint in the Summer of 1993. I now understand that Mr. JA has been located in Korea. Before Mr. JA is able to flee the country, I urge your government to act quickly to bring him into custody.

While I recognize that there is no extradition treaty between the Republic of Korea and the United States, I respectfully urge your government to consider seriously the extradition of Mr. JA to American authorities for trial at the situs of the alleged crime in the United States. If under Korean domestic law Mr. JA's extradition, deportation or expulsion is not possible, I request the opportunity to discuss with your government the alternative of having Mr. JA prosecuted in Korea.

Your assistance is greatly appreciated by the family of the victim, the people of New Jersey, and the people of the United States.

Sincerely,

ROBERT G. TORRICELLI
Member of Congress

were also taken by the Congressman of New Jersey. He sent a letter to the Korean Ambassador in the U.S., requesting assistance in bringing *JA*'s case to justice. The core content of the letter is as follows:

"While I recognize that there is no extradition treaty between the Republic of Korea and the United States, I respectfully urge your government to consider seriously the extradition of Mr. *JA* to American authorities for trial at the situs of the alleged crime in the United States. If under Korean domestic law Mr. *JA*'s extradition, deportation or expulsion is not possible, I request the opportunity to discuss with your government the alternative of having Mr. *JA* prosecuted in Korea."

Korea Denied the Extradition Request

The Korean government denied the request for extradition made by the U.S. Alternatively, Korean prosecutors tried to punish *JA* in Korea based on the mutal legal assistance request from the U.S.[88]

The U.S. government asked Korea to send *JA* back to the U.S. through extradition, deportation, or expulsion. However, deportation

---

88 Even though Korean Extradition Act was enacted in August 5, 1988, it did not have a provision concerning reciprocity, and the denial of extraditing a Korean national. Such provisions were included in December 14, 2005, through the amendment by Act No. 7727.

Article 4 (Reciprocity Principle)

Even though no extradition treaty is concluded, if it is guaranteed that any state requesting an extradition would comply with an extradition request of the Republic of Korea with respect to the same kind of or similar to extraditable crime, this Act shall be applicable.

Article 9 (Causes for Denial of Discretionary Extradition)

A criminal may not be extradited in cases falling under any of the following subparagraphs:

I. if the criminal is a citizen of the Republic of Korea; ...

was impossible because it is only applicable to foreigners, not nationals. And, expulsion was also impossible because Korea has never had such a system.

Extradition was denied because there was no extradition treaty between Korea and the U.S. at that time. The guarantee of reciprocity, which is necessary for extradition in the absence of a treaty, could not be expected from the U.S. because the U.S. has maintained its strong foreign policy of 'no treaty, no extradition.' Furthermore, *JA* was a national of Korea.[89] The denial was expressed through the following letter by the Korean Ambassador on December 5, 1994.

"It is not possible to extradite Mr. *JA* to the U.S. authorities in the absence of the relevant treaty between the two countries and extradition is not permitted to a Korean national. The Korean authorities, however, have indicated their readiness to consider the charges made against Mr. *JA* within the context of domestic statute and procedure when they receive an official request by the United States Department of Justice for such assistance and a full record of the U.S. investigation to date."

Without further discussion on the matter, an additional legal response from Korea was sent to the U.S. by way of a letter from the Korean Embassy, which was written by the Legal Attaché to the Director of the Office of International Affairs on February 2, 1995.

"According to the legal review of the Ministry of Justice, the extradition and deportation of the criminal as you requested is not possible under current Korean Law. As you know, there is no extradition treaty between our two countries, and the Korean

---

89 Principle of reciprocity and discretionary denial of a national could be applied.

Letter from Korean Ambassador to Congressman, December 5, 1994

EMBASSY OF THE REPUBLIC OF KOREA
WASHINGTON, D. C.

THE AMBASSADOR
SEUNG-SOO HAN

5 December, 1994

The Honorable Robert Torricelli
U.S. House of Representatives
Washington, DC 20515

Dear Congressman Torricelli:

I am writing in reference to our discussion of 18 October 1994 concerning the case against Mr. JA , the Korean-American who had allegedly fled to Korea after his release on bail.

As your staff has already been informed by my office, the Seoul Metropolitan Police did ultimately locate Mr. JA in Seoul, where he is currently under surveillance and subject to arrest on the charge of passport forgery. As I mentioned in our discussion, it is not possible to xtradite Mr. JA to the U.S. authorities in the absence of the relevant treaty between our two countries.

The Korean authorities have indicated their readiness to consider the charges made against Mr. JA in New Jersey within the context of domestic statute and procedure when they receive an official request by the United States Department of Justice for such assistance and a full record of the U.S. investigation to date.

I look forward to the expeditious resolution of this unfortunate case in an equitable and just manner.

Sincerely,

Seung Soo Han
Seung Soo-Han

Extradition Act requires the guarantee of reciprocity from the country in question in the absence of an extradition treaty in order to extradite a criminal to said country. We could not expect the reciprocal guarantee from the U.S. government. Furthermore, *JA* has the status of Korean citizenship and deportation is not applicable to nationals.

Korean government intends to punish the fled criminal in Korea. The Ministry of Justice is preparing to initiate the investigation and prosecute *JA* under the condition that the relevant U.S. authority pass over all the investigation documents and evidence necessary to prove the crime in court and it cooperates to have victim and possible witnesses testify in the prosecutor's office and the court."

Letter from the Korean Legal Attaché to the Director of OIA, Feb. 2, 1995

EMBASSY OF THE REPUBLIC OF KOREA
WASHINGTON, D. C.

February 2, 1995

Mr. George W. Proctor
Director
Office of International Affairs
Criminal Division
U.S. Department of Justice

Dear Mr. Proctor:

I have received the FAX letter of Jan. 23 regarding the __JA__ case. I immediately contacted the Ministry of Justice in Korea to respond your inquiry.

First of all, I have to inform you that the Ministry of Justice and Foreign Affairs has not yet received any formal request of mutual legal assistance concerning this case from the U.S. embassy in Seoul. Therefore, they are unable to make an official response to your request. As far as I know, the Ministry of Justice has already been fully apprised of the details and is well prepared to cooperate with your office in the __JA__ case.

According to the legal review of the Ministry of Justice, the extradition and deportation of the criminal as you requested is not possible under current Korean Law. As you know, there is no extradition treaty between our two countries, and the Korean Extradition Act requires the guarantee of reciprocity from the country in question in the absence of an extradition treaty in order to extradite a criminal to said country. We could not expect the reciprocal guarantee from the U.S. government. Furthermore, __JA__ has the status of Korean citizenship and deportation is not applicable to nationals.

Korean government intends to punish the fled criminal, __JA__, in Korea. The Ministry of Justice is preparing to initiate the investigation and prosecute the __JA__ case under the condition that the relevant U.S. authority pass over all the investigation documents and evidence necessary to prove the crime in court and it cooperate to have victim and possible witnesses testify in the prosecutor's office and the court.

I believe that the further cooperation between your office and Korean Ministry of Justice in the future will be needed to bring justice in this case. I will be pleased to contribute for the enhancement of such cooperate efforts

With Best Regards

Sincerely,

Kim Joon Gyu

Joon-Gyu Kim
Legal Attaché

Investigation in Korea

After jumping bail on March 24, 1994, *JA* was eventually located in Korea by the Seoul Metropolitan Police in November of 1994. *JA* was held under surveillance and subject to arrest on charges of passport forgery and drug possession by the Korean National Police. *JA* entered Korea with a false temporary travel certificate instead of his original passport which was confiscated by the court. *JA* had changed the spelling of his name, from *JAxx* to *CHAxx*, and thereafter applied to the Chicago Consulate of Korea for a temporary travel certificate to flee from the U.S.[90]

The Korean prosecutors' office initiated an investigation based on the MLA request from the U.S.

New Bergen County Prosecutor Withdrew Legal Assistance Request

Thereafter, a new prosecutor in Bergen County was appointed in May, and he withdrew the initiative launched by the former prosecutor and Congressman to have *JA* tried in Korea. Upon review, the Bergen County prosecutor felt that it would be too costly to cooperate and that

---

90 *JA* had gone to the Korean Consulate and said he lost his passport. He received a temporary travel certificate where he changed his name (*JAxx* → *CHAxx*). He was able to flee the U.S. and enter Korea by forging a false passport. Police arrested him on such charges as well as possession of drugs. While holding him, they continued on the rape investigation.

Letter from the Korean Legal Attaché to the Director of OIA, May 17, 1995

EMBASSY OF THE REPUBLIC OF KOREA
WASHINGTON, D. C.

May 17. 1995

Mr. George W. Proctor
Director, Office of International Affairs
Criminal Division
Department of Justice

Dear Mr. Proctor:

I have informed the Ministry of Justice in Korea as to your withdrawal of the request for the mutual legal assistance on **JA** 's case. I am writing this letter to inform you of the response from Korean government.

As you may know, the Korean Ministry of Justice, upon your request for the domestic punishment of fled criminal, had already started their preparation for the investigation and has been waiting for your cooperation with **JA** 's case. Although the U.S. withdrew the request, the Korean Ministry of Justice cannot retract its pursuance of the prosecution of **JA** 's case. Moreover, the Korean prosecutor's office is willing to take strong measures against such a blamable criminal activities as rape.

Although the crime was committed in the U.S., Mr. **JA** is a Korean citizen and can be punishable under the Korean criminal law. As a matter of principle, the Korean Government cannot let any known possible criminal go free without a proper trial.

In order to pursue the case, the Korean government needs cooperation from the U.S. in obtaining evidence and deposing the victim and the witnesses. Korean prosecutor's office has an intention to dispatch a Korean prosecutor to review this case and gather evidence for the trial in Korea.

I hope that the cooperation in this case could enhance a more amicable relationship between the two countries. Please, inform me of your opinion with regard to the proposal of Korean prosecutor's office and the future process of this case.

Thank you for your cooperation

Sincerely,

Joon - Gyu Kim
Legal Counselor

he could expect only a lenient sentence if *JA* was tried in Korea. The new Bergen County Prosecutor had expected to extradite *JA* in the future and to ultimately impose punishment in his own territory.

Korea Intended to Punish *JA* in Korea

Although the U.S. withdrew the request, the Korean Ministry of Justice decided not to retract its pursuance of the prosecution of *JA*'s case. The Korean prosecutors were willing to take strong measures against such deplorable criminal activities as rape and punish *JA* under the Korean criminal law.

However, Korean prosecutors in charge of the case needed cooperation from the U.S. in obtaining evidence and deposing the victim and witnesses. Accordingly, the Korean government in turn requested cooperation from the U.S. The Korean prosecutor even expressed an intention to dispatch a Korean prosecutor to the U.S. to review the case and gather evidence for the trial in Korea.

A few days later, a response from the Office of International Affairs of the Department of Justice was sent to the Legal Attaché in the Embassy of Korea. It stated one major clarification.

"Even though the U.S. Department of Justice and Department of State will make every effort to cooperate with the Korean authorities and reach satisfactory resolutions, they do not have jurisdiction over this matter or authority over decisions made by the State of New Jersey. In other words, the federal government has no legal authority to compel a branch of a state government to take a particular action.

Response letter from the OIA, May 26, 1995

U. S. Department of Justice

Washington, D.C. 20530

May 26, 1995

Kim, Joon-Gyu
Legal Attache
Embassy of Korea
2450 Mass. Avenue, N.W.
Washington, D.C. 20008

Dear Mr. Kim:

I am in receipt of your letter of May 17, 1995, advising of the Republic of Korea's position on the prosecution of Richard Jang in Korea.

As you are aware, this case is being prosecuted in the United States by the Bergen County, New Jersey, Prosecutor's Office. Under the U.S. constitutional system, the State of New Jersey (represented by the Bergen County Prosecutor's Office) has sovereign authority over the prosecution of this crime. The U.S. Departments of State and Justice do not have jurisdiction over this matter or authority over decisions made by the State of New Jersey in cases of this kind.

In this case, we have acted to assist the State of New Jersey in making requests to the Republic of Korea. Thus, we forwarded to you on behalf of Bergen County Prosecutor Jay Fahy a request for the extradition of JA , or in the alternative, his prosecution in Korea. Thereafter, Mr. Fahy's term expired and the new Acting Prosecutor requested that the Mr. Fahy's previous request be withdrawn. I have now forwarded a copy of your letter to the Director of the Division of Criminal Justice of the State of New Jersey, who has the authority to make the final decision in this matter. I believe he will respond to me in the near future. As soon as I have received his response, I will bring it to your immediate attention.

I wish to make one clarification. I will make every effort in this and all other state and local cases to present your government's views and attempt to reach satisfactory resolutions. However, the federal government has no legal authority to compel a branch of a state government to take a particular action in this type of criminal case. Thus, we ask your government to understand that the actions taken by the State of New Jersey in this matter are wholly independent of actions by the U.S. federal government.

In conclusion, I hope that this matter can be satisfactorily resolved, and I will contact you when I have received a response from the State of New Jersey. We look forward to continuing to build upon the spirit of cooperation that has been established between our two governments. I look forward to seeing you upon my return from Korea.

Sincerely,

George W. Proctor
Director
Office of International Affairs
Criminal Division

by: Kenneth J. Harris
~~Senior~~ Trial Attorney

Thus, the ensuing actions taken by the State of New Jersey would be wholly independent of actions by the U.S. federal government."[91]

The response from the U.S. federal government was that they were still willing to cooperate at the federal level even though it held limited power in this case and withdrawal of cooperation was separately decided by the county prosecutor.

Meeting Held between the State of New Jersey and Korean Authorities

Pursuant to several discussions between the State of New Jersey and the Office of International Affairs, the following letter was forwarded to the Legal Attaché in the Korean Embassy on July 14, 1995.

The Director of the Division of Criminal Justice of the State of New Jersey had proposed a meeting with the representatives from the Korean government and Department of Justice to discuss the Korean government's offer to prosecute *JA* in Korea. The representing

---

91 Federalism in the United States; The U.S. Constitution establishes a government based on federalism or the sharing of power between the national, and state (and local) governments. This power-sharing form of government is the opposite of centralized governments under which national government maintains total power. Sovereignty was considered indivisible and divided authority impossible. Federalism, however, split the atom of sovereignty, creating a system with two levels of strong, representative, and independent political power – the federal government and the states. (U.S. *Term Limits v. Thornton*,1995) Although federalism is embedded into the U.S. political and legal systems, tension between the federal government and the states is perpetually arising, and will probably continue to arise, as long as the U.S. system exists. (*McCulloch v. Maryland*,1817) Power has shifted back and forth between the federal and state governments, while the role of the courts in resolving federal-state conflicts continues to be sharply debated.

Proposal letter on meeting from the State of New Jersey, July 12, 1995

State of New Jersey
DEPARTMENT OF LAW AND PUBLIC SAFETY
DIVISION OF CRIMINAL JUSTICE
25 MARKET STREET
CN 085
TRENTON, NJ 08625-0085
TELEPHONE: (609) 984-6500

BORAH T. PORITZ
ORNEY GENERAL

TERRENCE P. FARLEY
DIRECTOR

July 12, 1995

United States Department of Justice
Criminal Division
Office of International Affairs
Washington, DC 20530

Attention: George W. Proctor, Director

Re: Prosecution of JA

Dear Director Proctor:

Pursuant to my several discussions with and letters from Kenneth J. Harris of your office, I am writing to let you know that both Acting Bergen County Prosecutor Charles Buckley and I would be willing to meet with representatives of the Republic of Korea and you or your staff to discuss the prosecution of JA for kidnapping, rape and other related charges.

As you are aware, there have been various discussions regarding the appropriate place for this prosecution. We would like to hear from the representatives of the Republic of Korea and your department before a final decision is made as to how and where to proceed with this case. Please call me at your convenience to arrange the meeting. I can be reached by telephone at (609) 984-0029.

Very truly yours,

Terrence P. Farley
Director

authorities met on September 12, 1995,[92] following subsequent arrangements to hold this meeting.

92 The following are the details regarding the meeting:
- Date: September 12, 1995

During the two hours of discussion, New Jersey officials were given information regarding the Korean criminal justice system, including potential punishment[93] and the likelihood of success of the prosecution instituted by Korean prosecutors.

The Bergen County Prosecutor had expected *JA* to be extradited from Korea after the signing of the extradition treaty between the two countries. Although the extradition treaty could be enforced in the future, there were still many problems in the extradition process of *JA* to the U.S. The process would take a long time to be completed. The statute of limitation, also a mandatory ground for the denial of extradition, had to be considered. Korea could also deny the request of U.S. because *JA* is a national, which is a discretionary denial ground of extradition. Also, if *JA* is convicted or acquitted in a trial in Korea, there would be the possibility of a double jeopardy defense, which could lead to a denial of request from Korea.[94]

Eventually, they agreed upon full cooperation regarding *JA*'s prosecution in Korea.[95] The Bergen County Prosecutor promised to send all the investigation documents as evidence for the trial in Korea.

- Location: 25 Market Street, Trenton, New Jersey (Capital of NJ)
- Venue: Division of Criminal Justice at Department of Law and Public Safety
- Participants
  Division of Criminal Justice, Director, Terrence P. Farley (Meeting Coordinator)
  Bergen County Prosecutor, Charles Buckley
  Office of International Affairs, Director, George Proctor
  Office of International Affairs, Senior Trial Attorney, Kenneth J. Harris
  Legal Attaché (Representative of Korea), Joon Gyu Kim

93 The expected sentence of *JA* in Korea was communicated to Bergen County Prosecutors as 7-10 years imprisonment.

94 Double jeopardy is a mandatory denial ground between Korea and the U.S.

95 Korean Legal Attaché was able to erase any doubts concerning the issues raised by the participants.

Investigation and Prosecution of *JA*

In the following year, the case entered a new phase as the Violent Crime Division of the Seoul District Prosecutors' Office arrested *JA* on charges of kidnapping, rape and other related offences on January

Article from *North Jersey* on January 17, 1996

NORTH JERSEY

■ BERGEN 3
■ COMMUNITY BRIEFING 4
■ LAW & ORDER 5
■ EDITORIALS/OPINION 6

WEDNESDAY, JANUARY 17, 1996 — SECTION NJ

Man admits to Bergen rape

S. Korean faces 15-year term in homeland

By JIM CONSOLI
Staff Writer

A South Korean national accused of kidnapping and raping a woman in Bergen County has confessed to the crimes in his homeland and is facing a maximum 15-year prison term there, South Korean authorities said Tuesday.

JA , 20, admitted his role in abducting a Palisades Park woman from Yaohan Plaza in Edgewater in July 1993, then repeatedly sexually assaulting her with an accomplice in a Fort Lee motel, said Joon Gyu Kim, legal attaché at the South Korean Embassy in Washington.

Jang "made the confession in front of a [Korean] prosecutor," Kim said, adding that Jang is expected to be indicted by month's end.

But acting Bergen County Prosecutor Charles R. Buckley said Tuesday that South Korea's prosecution of Jang will have no impact on the outstanding 37-count indictment hanging over his head in New Jersey.

"If he returns to the United States, we'll pick him up and prosecute him," Buckley said.

Jang could face a prison sentence of more than 100 years if convicted on the charges in Bergen County.

Jang, who lived with his mother in Leonia for a decade, fled to South Korea after his father, a millionaire businessman, posted $350,000 cash bail for him in early 1994. His flight occurred after Superior Court Judge Sybil R. Moses lowered Jang's $1 million bail.

Joon Gyu Kim said Jang would be indicted in South Korea based on his confession and information contained in investigative reports his government obtained from the Bergen County Prosecutor's Office.

Jang, who confessed after his Jan. 9 arrest in Seoul, is being held without bail at a detention center in Seoul, he said. In his homeland, Jang is known as Chang Jun-Ho.

His arrest came about a year after South Korean officials acknowledged to the U.S. Department of Justice that Jang was back in their country.

One area Korean-American leader on

See CONFESSION Page NJ-3

CONFESSION

From Page NJ-1

Tuesday pressed for Jang's return to the U.S.

Jang "deserves to be punished severely for what he did, but it would be better off if he was punished in Bergen County rather than Korea," said Jason Kim, vice chairman of the Korean-American Voters Association in Englewood Cliffs.

He said he hoped Jang is given the maximum 15-year sentence in South Korea.

"It would give a message to anybody, whether they are Korean or American, that nobody can get away with a crime by fleeing our country," Jason Kim said.

But on Tuesday, Joon Gyu Kim reiterated his country's stance that it would not extradite or deport Jang because South Korea has no extradition treaty with the U.S.

In May, Buckley dropped an initiative launched by former Bergen County Prosecutor John J. Fahy and Rep. Robert G. Torricelli, D-Englewood, to have Jang tried in South Korea.

An accomplice in the case pleaded guilty last year.

Buckley said he feared Jang would receive a lenient sentence if convicted in South Korea and then could argue in the United States that trying him again here would constitute double jeopardy.

However, legal experts said the chances of a successful double jeopardy argument are remote.

"The risk of double jeopardy applying is unlikely," said Brian Neary, a Hackensack defense attorney. "[U.S.] constitutional issues are usually restricted to the borders of the U.S."

An accomplice in the case, Jun-sung Kim, pleaded guilty last year to charges of kidnapping and sexual assault. Kim is serving an 18-year prison term with no chance of parole for eight years.

9, 1996. Thereafter, on January 16, *JA* confessed his crimes to the prosecutors[96] while he was being held without bail at the detention center in Seoul. He was subsequently prosecuted on January 27, 1996. The charges against *JA* consisted of 14 counts.

The accomplice in the case, *Kim*, had already pled guilty in 1995 to charges of kidnapping and sexual assault. He was serving an eighteen year prison term with no chance of parole for eight years in the U.S.

Korea Requested Legal Assistance to the U.S.

On January 30, 1996, the Korean Ministry of Justice sent a letter of request for legal assistance[97] to the United States. Authenticated investigation documents were requested as the Korean authorities had believed that documentary evidence was necessary and sufficient for a successful trial of *JA*, in addition to his confession. In this letter, Korea requested the following documents to the U.S.:

- Statement made by *JA*
- Judgment setting out the conviction and the sentence imposed against the accomplice
- Expert diagnostic evaluation of injuries sustained by the victim issued by a doctor or other appropriate authorities
- Any other evidence that would help establish the case in hand.

96 According to the Korean legal procedure, unofficial investigation documents are admissible as evidence if the defendant agrees with the contents.

97 It was initiated by the Korean prosecutors.

Request for Legal Assistance by the Ministry of Justice in Korea, January 30, 1996

MINISTRY OF JUSTICE
REPUBLIC OF KOREA

30 January, 1996

To : Office of International Affairs
Department of Justice
United States

Re: Request for Assistance in Criminal Matters

The Ministry of Justice of the Republic of Korea, Prosecution Bureau, Fourth Prosecution Division, the competent authority of the Republic of Korea for the purpose of requesting legal assistance in criminal matters from the foreign States, requests the assistance of appropriate authorities in the United States regarding a criminal investigation of **JA** who is charged with having kidnapped and raped **OOO** in collaboration with **XXX** in New Jersey on or about during and between July 31, 1993 and August 1, 1993.

In response to your request for the prosecution of **JA** in the Korean court, the Violent Crime Division(VCD) of the Seoul District Public Prosecutors Office arrested **JA** on charges of kidnapping, rape and other related offenses on January 9 and filed an indictment with the court on January 27.

I enclose a letter of request for assistance in obtaining evidence in the United States. The VCD believes that the documentary evidence requested in the letter is indispensable to a successful prosecution of Jun Ho Jang.

In case that **JA** may plead not guilty in the trial court although **JA** confessed to the rape charges during the interrogation, the VCD might make a supplemental request for making arrangements for the victim or the accomplice to appear before the court and testify to the charges filed against **JA**

JA's Trial in Korea

During the trial, *JA* neither pled guilty nor confessed his charge. Even though *JA* made a full confession regarding the above charges during the investigation stage, he denied repeatedly the charges against him, claiming that he had not participated in the rape of the Japanese female. Furthermore, he revoked his confession to the prosecutor under the advice of a defense lawyer. He attempted to discredit his confession before the prosecutor by claiming that he signed the statement without fully understanding its contents due to his poor ability to speak and read Korean.

According to the Korean criminal procedure, prosecutors have to present evidence in the trial to prove *JA*'s charges if the defendant does not consent to the use of evidence in the investigation document provided by prosecutors. *JA* and his defense attorney denied even the authenticity of the statement made by the female victim, filed in the United States. Under the Korean Code of Criminal Procedure, the general rule is that hearsay evidence, including the statement of the witness recorded by an investigator, is not admissible unless the witness appears before the court and testifies to the authenticity of the statement.

2nd MLA Request of Korea to the U.S.

Eventually, Korean authorities made a supplemental request for legal assistance[98] on May 23, 1996. They requested testimonies of the witness and the accomplice as they seemed to be crucial evidence in the criminal trial of *JA*.

This request was about permitting the witnesses to appear before the court and to testify to the charges filed against *JA*.

At this stage, the problems were:

(1) Where these testimonies could be taken (the U.S. *vs*. Korea),

(2) By whom these testimonies should be taken (Korean Judge *vs*. U.S. Judge).

The Korean court requested that both the witness and accomplice travel to Korea and testify before the Korean judge.

U.S. Efforts to Accept Korean Request for Legal Assistance

Thereafter, on June 18, 1996, the U.S. Department of Justice sent a final response with regards to the Korean government's request for legal assistance. The U.S. response was that it wanted to cooperate but had no legal authority to compel the victim or accomplice to travel to Korea and testify.

The Justice Department of the U.S. said,

"I am pleased to report that both witnesses are prepared to provide testimony in the Korean prosecution of this case. However, neither witness will be able to travel to Korea to give testimony; thus,

98 It was initiated by the Korean judge.

2nd Request for Legal Assistance by the Korean Ministry of Justice, May 23, 1996

MINISTRY OF JUSTICE
REPUBLIC OF KOREA

May 23, 1996

To : Office of International Affairs
Department of Justice
United States

Re: Request for Assistance in Criminal Matters

The Ministry of Justice of the Republic of Korea, Prosecution Bureau, Fourth Prosecution Division, the competent authority of the Republic of Korea for the purpose of requesting legal assistance in criminal matters from the foreign States, requests the assistance of appropriate authorities in the United States regarding a criminal trial of JA , who is being on trial in the Seoul District Court for the charges as indicated in our previous request dated February 26. I would like to take this opportunity to appreciate your prompt response to our previous request for obataining the authenticated copy of documents relating to the investigation of JA in the United States.

I enclose herewith a letter of request from the Seoul District Public Prosecutors' Office seeking, *inter alia*, assistance in obtaining witnesses to be used in the trial proceeded against JA . The Seoul District Public Prosecutors' Office believes that testimony by the witness is very important to a successful prosecution of JA .

The Republic of Korea appreciates the cooperation and aid it has received in the past from the Government of the United States in the area of international law if agreeable to Korean authorities, the U.S. Department of Justice is prepared to make immediate arrangements for the testimony of these witnesses to be taken in the U.S."

Whether they testify in Korea depended on their own willingness. Both the victim and accomplice wanted to provide testimony for the punishment of *JA*. But they were not willing to travel to Korea. The victim was unwilling because she was a Japanese American, a young lady, and a rape victim. The accomplice was a Korean American and was ashamed to travel to his homeland in custody.

The victim indicated that she "definitely wishes to cooperate in bringing Mr. *JA* to justice but is unwilling to make a long journey to Korea, far from familiar surroundings and support."

If a witness is unwilling to travel to a foreign country to give testimony, under U.S. law, the witness cannot be compelled to do so. As for the accomplice who was serving a lengthy term of imprisonment in the U.S. for his role in this crime, the Department of Justice lacked domestic legal authority to transfer to Korea the person in custody to give testimony without his consent.

In this situation, the U.S. proposed, based on the inability of these witnesses to appear in Korea, to prepare full and immediate assistance in arranging for the taking of such testimonies in the U.S, should the Korean government decide that testimonies in the U.S. was feasible.

Further information is provided on the letter from the Director of OIA in the U.S. Department of Justice to the Korean Judge of the Seoul District Court. It stated,

"In terms of the procedure that would be used in such a case, under our legal assistance law – Title 28, United States Code, Section

Letter by the DOJ in response to Korean request for MLA, June 18, 1996

U. S. Department of Justice

Criminal Division

Washington, D.C. 20530

FFT:LCB:KJH
182-

June 18, 1996

VIA TELEFAX

Mr. Kim, Joon-Gyu
Legal Attache
Embassy of Korea
2450 Massachusetts Avenue N.W.
Washington, D.C. 20008

Re: Request for Legal Assistance by the Republic of Korea to the United States of America in Prosecution of JA

Dear Mr. Kim:

In response to your government's requests for legal assistance in the above-captioned case, dated February 26 and May 23, 1996, I wish to provide the following information concerning the evidence you have requested.

With regard to your request for witness testimony, the United States Attorney's Office for the District of New Jersey has met with both XXX, the victim of the crime, and OOO, the co-defendant who is currently imprisoned in New Jersey for his role in the crime. I am pleased to report that both witnesses are prepared to provide testimony in the Korean prosecution of this case. However, neither witness will be able to travel to Korea to give testimony; thus, if agreeable to Korean authorities, the United States Department of Justice is prepared to make immediate arrangements for the testimony of these witnesses to be taken in the United States.

At the time that the U.S. Attorney's office interviewed Ms. XXX, she indicated that she wishes to provide her testimony in the United States, but is unwilling to travel to the Republic of Korea. Ms. XXX definitely wishes to cooperate in bringing JA to justice. However, in our experience, it is not unusual for a victim of such a serious attack to have extreme reluctance

Letter to the Korean Judge with regard to the MLA Request, July 2, 1996.

U. S. Department of Justice
Criminal Division

Washington, D.C. 20530

FFT:LCB:KJH
182-

July 2, 1996

VIA TELEFAX TO KOREAN EMBASSY
AND VIA DIPLOMATIC CHANNELS

Judge Choi, Jeong Su
Seoul District Court
1701-1 Seocho-Dong
Seocho-Gu
Seoul, Korea

Re: Request for Legal Assistance by the Seoul District Court to the United States of America in Prosecution of JA, Case Number 96 Ko Hap 54

Dear Judge Choi:

My name is Kenneth Harris, and I am an attorney with the United States Department of Justice, Office of International Affairs, the Central Authority for processing legal assistance requests in criminal matters between the Republic of Korea and the United States. I write this letter in response to your request for legal assistance in the above-captioned case, dated May 27, 1996.

It is my understanding that, in your request, you ask for the following types of assistance: 1) That two witnesses, the victim XXX and the co-defendant OOO, be invited to testify in this case in the Seoul District Court on July 3, 1996 (their travel expenses will be borne by Korea); and 2) if the witnesses are unable to attend, that the testimony be taken in a United States court and be forwarded to Korea for use in your proceedings.

At the outset, let me state that the reason I was not able to respond earlier to your request is that your legal assistance request apparently arrived at the Korean Embassy in Washington,

1782 – the United States District Court for the District of New Jersey would normally issue an order appointing a "commissioner," meaning a representative of the court, to take the testimony. Normally, the commissioner would be an Assistant United States Attorney.

The Assistant United States Attorney would facilitate the taking of testimony in this matter; in addition, as representative of the court he or she would ensure that the request were carried out in compliance with U.S. law and the directions of the U.S. District Court.

In addition, you should be aware that our legal assistance law has flexibility regarding the procedures that may be used to ensure that the testimony is taken by the methods that comply with legal requirements in the country where the testimony is to be used… The U.S. District Court could also order that the testimony be recorded by audio and video-tape, if you request."

Testimony Hearing of the Witness in the U.S.

After deciding to hold the testimony hearing in the U.S., the following letters were exchanged between the U.S. Department of Justice and the Seoul District Court. Details regarding the legal assistance were discussed.

The U.S. strongly encouraged that a Korean judicial official travel to the U.S. to directly participate in taking the testimonies. However, the Korean Judge was unable to travel to the U.S. to question the victim and the accomplice, due to an overload of pending cases.

Therefore, it was suggested that a U.S. Commissioner should

Letters exchanged between the DOJ of the U.S. and Seoul District Court (1)

U. S. Department of Justice

Criminal Division

Washington, D.C. 20530

FFT:LCB:KJH
182-

October 24, 1996

VIA TELEFAX TO KOREAN EMBASSY
AND VIA DIPLOMATIC CHANNELS

Judge Choi, Jeong Su
Seoul District Court
1701-1 Seocho-Dong
Seocho-Gu
Seoul, Korea

Re: Request for Legal Assistance by the Seoul District Court to the United States of America in Prosecution of JA, Case Number 96 Ko Hap 54

Dear Judge Choi:

Thank you for your recent request, a copy of which I today received from the Korean embassy. As I understand your request, you wish to have U.S. officials interview two witnesses -- the victim XXX and the co-defendant OOO -- using the questionnaire sent in your prior request for legal assistance dated May 27, 1996, and that the answers be recorded and forwarded to you for use as evidence at the trial of this matter. From your request, it also appears that it may be possible for a Korean judicial official to travel to the United States to directly take part in the questioning of the witnesses.

The United States would strongly encourage you to arrange for a Korean judicial official (and any other appropriate persons) to travel to the United States to directly participate in the taking of this testimony. In our experience in conducting international legal assistance, it is infrequent that foreign requests for testimony of critical witnesses for use at trial are carried out by U.S. officials without direct participation of a law enforcement official or officials from the requested State.

take the testimony. It was also finally decided that the testimonies of the victim and accomplice were to be video-taped in full, and certified documents and videotape of the testimonies were to be transferred to the Korean court as evidence of the *JA* case. The Seoul District Court forwarded a questionnaire, which could be a reasonable compromise for obtaining the substantive information they needed without their presence in the examination of the testimonies.

After further deliberation, the testimony hearing of the accomplice was held in the New Jersey District Court in Newark on December 10, 1996. The United States strongly recommended the presence of Korean judicial officers during the testimony hearing. They said,

"the U.S. commissioner may not be fully aware of the issues most important for correct resolution of this matter under Korean law, or the manner in which the questioning should be conducted in order to meet all Korean legal requirements. The participation of a Korean judicial official familiar with the case can fully ensure that the testimony of these critical witnesses is carried out in the manner most useful for the purposes of a trial in Korea."

The testimony was taken by an Assistant U.S. Attorney, who was assigned as the commissioner by the court. The Legal Attaché of the Korean Embassy also went to Newark and met with the commissioner before the proceeding to explain the questions in need and the Korean legal system, including the admissibility of evidence under Korean law.

On December 16, 1996, the testimony of the victim was taken at her residence in New Jersey. The victim, however, asked for certain assurances prior to giving her testimony, which the Korean

Letters exchanged between the DOJ of the U.S. and Seoul District Court (2)

Seoul District Court
Republic of Korea

November 20, 1996

Kenneth J. Harris, Esq.
Senior Trial Attorney
Office of International Affairs
United States Department of Justice

Request for Legal Assistance

Dear Mr. Harris:

Thanks very much for your letter of October 24, 1996 regarding defendant JA . We appreciate your cooperation, and your kind advice on the best procedure for questioning the witnesses is well taken.

We understand that it is infrequent for you to take the testimony without participation by the law enforcement official of the assistance-requesting country. Unfortunately, however, we are unable to directly participate in questioning the witnesses. At this time of the year, Korean courts are typically overloaded with pending cases, and we can hardly be away from the court. This situation prevents us from flying to the United States for examining the witnesses.

We have evaluated the potential impact of our absence in the examination, and concluded that the questionnaire that we forwarded you in May should be a reasonable compromise for obtaining the substantive information we need. Will you kindly take the testimony of the witnesses for each question in the questionnaire, and forward us a document in which the answers are recorded? If permissible under U.S. law, we would also appreciate your video-recording the testimony and forwarding us a copy of the video-cassette.

Regarding the procedure and formality of examination, please make sure that, on the last page of the document recording the answer, (1) the U.S. commissioner who questions the witnesses write his name and title and sign the document, and (2) the witness also write his name and sign the document. Except the above identification requirement, you may follow your own procedure and standard in questioning the witnesses.

We look forward to a response as prompt as practicable. We would be most thankful if the result of the examination is made available to us by December 15, 1996.

Sincerely yours,

Choi, Jeong-Su
Judge, Chief of the Trial Division
Seoul District Court

Commissioner, Assistant U.S. Attorney

Legal Attaché, Korean Embassy[99]

Government accepted. She requested:

1) That the courtroom in which the trial is held in Korea be cleared of the general public during the showing of the video tape,
2) That the videotape not be made public, and
3) That she not be requested to give her testimony again with regard to these proceedings.

As a final result of the proceeding, two copies of the recorded video tape with the attached stenographic transcript were obtained and forwarded to Korea based on the MLA request. The following documents were provided as certification.

99 The photos above were taken during the actual proceeding of taking testimony on the accomplice.

Certified Transcript of the Testimony (1)

United States
Department of Justice

Washington, D.C., December 18, 19 96

To ... hom these presents shall come, Greeting:

That Frances Fragos Townsend whose name is signed

to t... panying paper, is now, and was at the time of signing the same,

...ffice of International Affairs, Criminal Division, U.S. Department

o... /ashington, D.C.

duly commissioned and qualified.

In ... hereof, *I*, Janet Reno

Attorney General of the United States, have hereunto caused the Seal of the Department of Justice to be affixed and my name to be attested by the Deputy Assistant Attorney General for Administration, of the said Department on the day and year first above written.

Janet Reno
Attorney General

By Michael J. Roper
Deputy Assistant Attorney General for Administration

Certified Transcript of the Testimony (2)

IN THE UNITED STATES DISTRICT COURT
FOR THE DISTRICT OF NEW JERSEY
CIVIL ACTION NO. 96-429

IN RE:	: (Videotaped)
IN THE CRIMINAL MATTER OF	: SWORN
	: STATEMENT OF
JA	: OOO KIM

TRANSCRIPT of testimony as taken by and before ROSEMARY MARINO, a Certified Shorthand Reporter and Notary Public of the State of New Jersey, at the U.S. POST OFFICE and COURTHOUSE, Walnut Street, Newark, New Jersey, on Tuesday, December 10, 1996, commencing at 12:23 in the afternoon.

A P P E A R A N C E S:

V. GRADY O'MALLEY, ESQ.
Senior Litigation Counsel
Assistant United States Attorney
970 Broad Street
Newark, New Jersey 07102
(201) 645-2700

ALSO PRESENT:

Joon-Gyu Kim
Legal Attache

Yong Kim
Interpreter

Certified Transcript of the Testimony (3)

UNITED STATES DISTRICT COURT FOR THE
DISTRICT OF NEW JERSEY

IN RE: Letter of Request from the Seoul Ministry of Justice, Seoul Public Prosecutors' Office, Republic of Korea for Assistance in the Criminal Matter of JA

No. 96-429

CERTIFICATION

I, V. Grady O'Malley, Assistant United States Attorney, Senior Litigation Counsel, in the District of New Jersey, having been appointed Commissioner by Order of this Court on June 19, 1996, for the purpose of taking evidence in accordance with the request of the Seoul Public Prosecutors' Office, certify that attached hereto are the following documents and items of evidence obtained pursuant to that Order; namely,

(1) a true and accurate statement taken from the victim on August 1, 1993, taken by the Bergen County, New Jersey Prosecutor's Office and affirmed as truthful on December 16, 1996.

(2) a true and accurate video recording of the statement taken from the victim , on December 16, 1996, at her residence in New Jersey, U.S.A.;

(3) a true and accurate statement taken from co-defendant OOO on August 6, 1993, taken by the Bergen County Prosecutor's Office and affirmed by OOO Kim as truthful on December 10, 1996.

(4) a true and accurate video recording (with certification) of the statement taken from co-defendant OOO Kim on December 10, 1996, at the Federal Courthouse in Newark, New Jersey, U.S.A.;

(5) a true and correct transcript of the stenographic statement taken from co-defendant OOO Kim on December 10, 1996 at the Federal Courthouse in Newark, New Jersey, U.S.A.;

(6) a true and accurate copy of a 3 page plea form executed and signed by co-defendant OOO Kim on November 7, 1993 before the Honorable Sybil R. Moses, Superior Court Judge, Bergen County, New Jersey, U.S.A.

(7) a true and correct stenographic transcript of the tatement taken from the victim on December 16, 1996 at her esidence in New Jersey, U.S.A.;

(8) a true and accurate copy of the Judgment of Conviction for OOO Kim as certified by seal of the Bergen County, New Jersey Clerk's Office.

(9) an original "authentication of judgment" regarding the plea and sentencing of OOO Kim signed by the Honorable Sybil R. Moses, Superior Court Judge, Bergen County, New Jersey, U.S.A..

(10) a certified copy of the medical records of the victim received pursuant to subpoena from Englewood New Jersey Hospital & Medical Center.

I also certify that the sworn statement of Ms. the victim was taken on December 16, 1996 in her residence at her specific request. The victim was also questioned in a fashion which specifically considered the traumatic impact that reliving, in detail, the events of July 31, 1993 and August 1, 1993, would have upon her. Yet, the victim was also questioned with a view towards obtaining sufficient detail to fulfill the evidentiary requests made by the Prosecutor's Office and the Seoul District Court.

V. Grady O'Malley
V. GRADY O'MALLEY
Commissioner

Dated: This 17th day of December 1996.

Ruling by the Korean Supreme Court

The videotaped testimony was very essential to this case. The evidence obtained from the U.S. by way of mutual legal assistance was adopted and admitted in the Korean court. In trial court, *JA* was found guilty and sentenced to ten years in prison. He appealed and the sentence was reduced to seven years in prison in appellate court. However, the final appeal by *JA* was denied by the Supreme Court.[100]

The video-recorded testimonies of the witnesses were paramount in bringing *JA* to justice through mutual legal assistance between Korea and the U.S.

This case set two new precedents in the Korean Supreme Court:

(1) Using video-taped testimony for the first time in court

(2) Using investigation documents by foreign officers[101] in court.

It is also noteworthy in this case that 'statement, deposition, and interrogatory produced by a competent law enforcement agency of a foreign country may be considered as admissible evidence in the Courts of Korea.'

---

100 Korean Supreme Court Judgment on July 25, 1997 (대법원 1997. 7. 25. 선고 97 도 1351 판결)

101 Authenticated by Mutual Legal Assistance.

Summary of the Supreme Court Judgment

– Issue –

Whether the [1] court documents and statements made by a competent law enforcement agency of a foreign country; and [2] an interrogatory statement and deposition record made by an accused and produced by the U.S. Court, following the request made in accordance with the Mutual Legal Assistance in Criminal Matters, are considered as admissible evidence in the courts of Korea.

– Judgment –

It is determined that the statement, deposition, and interrogatory produced by a competent law enforcement agency of a foreign country may be considered as admissible evidence in the Courts of Korea under Article 314 of the Criminal Act only when the following requirements are satisfied:

(a) The deponent is not in a position to appear and provide his or her statement at the court hearing due to his or her death, illness or other acceptable reasons;

(b) There is no reasonable ground to believe that there was falsehood or fabrication in the statement and when conducting interrogatory and deposition procedures; and

(c) There are sufficient evidence and surrounding circumstances to suggest that the contents of the statements are credible and voluntarily given by the deponent.

Successful Case of Mutual Legal Assistance But ..

The *JA* case is a successful example of mutual legal assistance. But, it presents us with many problems of cooperation in criminal matters.

First, MLA process takes too long. As shown in the *JA* case, it took more than three years to punish the fled criminal and more than two years for the MLA request to be realized. There are also too many formalities required in diplomacy, which causes unnecessary delay in cooperation.

Second, despite the success of legal assistance, there was a disparity in the punishment of *JA* and the accomplice, who were tried and sentenced in different courts of different countries. *JA*, the main culprit of the crime, was sentenced to seven years in prison in the Korean Court, while the accomplice who was less involved in the crime received eighteen years in prison in the U.S. Court.

Nevertheless, there is a positive note to point out. The testimony video which was recorded in a foreign country opened the doors to a new way of cooperation in the field of legal assistance. We can further hope for the adoption of more enhanced and efficient tools such as video conferences and emails for cooperation in the future.

Case Timetable

Date	Event
1993. 7. 31	*JA* and accomplice abducted the female victim to a motel where she is repeatedly raped and sexually abused at gun point. [New Jersey, U.S.]
1993. 8	*JA* was arrested by the U.S. authorities.
1994. 3. 24	*JA* jumped bail.
1994. 11	*JA* was located in Korea.
1994. 11. 17	U.S. made an extradition request to Korea.
1994. 12. 5	Korea denied the extradition request, but intended to punish *JA* in Korea.
1995. 9. 12	Meeting between Korean Embassy and New Jersey authorities.
1996. 1. 9	*JA* was arrested and prosecuted in Korea for charges of kidnapping and rape.
1996. 1. 30	Korea made a mutual legal assistance request to the U.S.
1996. 5. 21	Second request for legal assistance by Korea to the U.S.
1996. 6. 18	U.S. accepted Korea's request for legal assistance.
1996. 12. 10	Testimony of the accomplice was recorded in U.S. District Court of New Jersey.
1996. 12. 16	Testimony of the victim was recorded in her residence in New Jersey.
Trial in Korea	In Korea, *JA* was found guilty and sentenced to ten years in prison.
	JA's sentence was reduced to seven years in appellate court.
	The Supreme Court denied the re-appeal by *JA* and the sentence of seven years in prison was confirmed.

4. Nigerian Drug Dealer Case

Summary of the Case

Defendant *CO*, a Nigerian drug dealer, enticed Koreans into becoming his means of delivering drugs. After unsuccessful attempts by Korea to extradite him from Germany and Denmark, *CO* was eventually caught and extradited from China to Korea. It is noteworthy that China was a non-concerned Party in relation to this crime. Also, mutual legal assistance was successfully displayed through collaborative efforts to convict *CO* in the Korean court.

Nigerian Drug Dealer Enticed Koreans

CO was known to be a ringleader of an international drug organization, and his primary place of operation was concentrated in Europe. After realizing that Korea is a drug-free nation, he gradually began to move his strategic base to Korea from the late 1990s. He started taking Korean language classes in 1998 and he became quite fluent after two years.

Around June 30, 1999, his thorough preparation started expanding as he set up a bogus company in Seoul, Korea. While disguising it as a shop for dealing used motorcycle components, 'Fechinco Korea' started operating as a middle ground for illicit drug trafficking. In order to attain his foremost goal, he then began searching for his means of delivering the drugs.

His targets were mainly young women and he began to approach them with his skillful manner and fluency in Korean, English, and six other languages. Expensive suits and luxurious accessories added credibility to his words and behavior as he introduced himself as an American businessman. He normally met them in night clubs and he boasted his success in the current clothing trade businesses. He constantly displayed his lavish spending to them as he seduced them by giving them expensive gifts and enticing them with free trips overseas. Without much doubt and hesitation, the young women began to cooperate with *CO*'s evil schemes.

Under the belief that they were carrying samples of clothing and were receiving a commission fee for their delivery, the Korean women began to carry specially-manufactured luggage filled with drugs to various destinations abroad.[102] The smuggled drugs, ranging from 40 kilograms of cocaine to several hundred kilograms of marijuana, were sent to the Netherlands, Denmark, U.K., Japan, Peru, and many other places.

---

102 As of September 2003, *CO* expanded his range of drug carriers to include men and older-aged people.

List of Korean drug carriers who worked under *CO*

Date	Name (Sex/ Birth)	Contents (Route)
2002. 5. 17	PARK (F, 1981)	Cocaine 4 kg (Peru → Netherland)
2002. 6. 27	LEE (F, 1986), JUN (F, 1986) SON (F, 1987)	Marijuana 40 kg (Thailand → Korea → Japan)
2002. 6. 29	KANG (F, 1980)	Marijuana 40 kg (Korea → Japan)
2002. 11. 10	MOON (F, 1982) CHU (F, 1981)	Cocaine 12 kg (Peru → Brazil)
2002. 11. 24	BANG (F, 1978) TAE (F, 1978)	Cocaine 10 kg (Guyana → U.K.)
2002. 11. 29	PARK, K. (F, 1974)	Cocaine 6 kg (Peru → Netherland)
2003. 9. 10	YOON (M, 1979)	Cocaine 7 kg (Peru → Denmark) * Served 7 years in Denmark.
2005. 4. 24	PARK, C. (M, 1965)	Cocaine 8 kg (Argentina → U.K.) * Released due to insufficient evidence.
2005. 8. 27	KIM (F, 1967)	Cocaine 4.3 kg (Peru → France) * Served 2 years in France.
2006. 6. 14	CHOI (M, 1948) LEE, S. (M, 1953)	Cocaine 9.8 kg (Peru → Spain) * CHOI was sentenced 6 years and 8 months in Peru and released afterwards. LEE is serving 9 years in Peru.
2006. 9. 11	SEU (M, 1976) LEE, B. (M, 1968)	Cocaine 3 kg and 2 kg (Brazil → Spain) * SEU and LEE are serving 9 years in Spain.
2006. 11. 9	JEONG (M, 1963)	Cocaine 9 kg (Argentina → Spain) * Served 4 years and 2 months in Argentina.
2006. 11. 16	KIM, S (M, 1975)	Cocaine 6 kg (Argentina → Spain) * Served 4 years and 9 months in Argentina.
2006. 12. 25	KIM, J. (M, 1961)	Cocaine 8.5 kg (Brazil → Spain) * Serving 10 years in Spain.
2007. 2. 4	CHEON (M, 1957)	Cocaine 2.4 kg (Brazil → Peru → Spain) * Serving 6 years and 8 months in Peru.

CO's victims automatically became criminals of drug trafficking and upon subsequent conviction in the respective countries, they are currently serving or have completed serving prison terms ranging from two to ten years in foreign prisons.

Flow Chart of the Case Proceedings

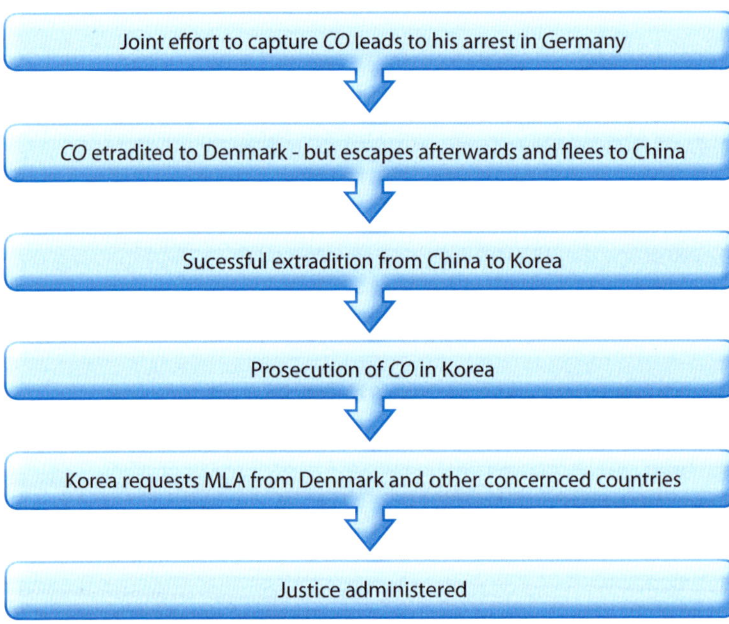

Joint Efforts Result in *CO*'s Arrest in Germany

Since narcotic drugs are strictly prohibited in Korea, the fact that *CO* used Koreans to smuggle drugs internationally and utilized them as drug carriers caused much disturbance and alarm in the Korean society. As such, the Korean Prosecution Service and the National Intelligence

Service in Korea began to track down *CO* and his members in 2000.

Feeling pressure from the investigation in Korea, *CO* fled to Germany on June 30, 2002 with a forged passport and continued his crime against Korean travelers, once again enticing them into carrying drugs. Realizing the severity of the issue, the Ministry of Foreign Affairs and the National Police Agency of Korea were also called into the joint effort of capturing *CO*.

Thereafter, on October 21, 2003, the joint effort by the Korean authorities paid off, as *CO* was arrested by the Interpol at the Frankfurt Airport in Germany.

Extradition of *CO* to Denmark
– But *CO* Escaped to China

Despite the extradition request from Korea to Germany, *CO* was extradited to Denmark on February 17, 2004. The extradition to Denmark had been decided due to the pending case of a Korean college student who had been caught in Denmark for smuggling 10kg of cocaine in August 2003.

What seemed like a successful outcome of the pursuit, however, entered into a new phase, as *CO* escaped from the Danish detention center named Aarhus on May 28, 2004. *CO*'s escape left the Korean Prosecution Service frustrated as they had hoped the prosecution of *CO* would lead to the collapse of the Nigerian drug gang in Korea and help reduce the sentence of Korean drug carriers serving their time in foreign prisons.

Successful Extradition from China to Korea

After a long period of hiding overseas, *CO* was eventually located in China. The fugitive had entered China with a forged passport around April of 2005. He was found in Shenyang teaching the Korean language to Nigerians and once again attempting to use Koreans for delivering drugs.

Fortunately, he was captured by the Chinese Police Agency in February 2007. In accordance with the *Treaty on Extradition between the Republic of Korea and the People's Republic of China*,[103] the Korean government requested the extradition of *CO*. On October 2007, the High Court of Liaoning, China, approved the request.

As a result of this arduous process, *CO* returned to Korea via Korean Air departing from Shenyang on September 11, 2008. It took almost six years for him to reset his foot in Korea.

Prosecution of *CO* in Korea

More than six years of relentless pursuit by the Korean authority, which began in 2002 and involved three separate extradition requests to Germany, Denmark, and China, finally paid off and led to the extradition of *CO* to Korea.

103 Signed in Seoul on October 18, 2000 and entered into force on April 12, 2002.

The letter from China to Korea approving the request for extradition, July 3, 2008

中 华 人 民 共 和 国 外 交 部

（2008）部条字第169号

大韩民国驻华大使馆：

中华人民共和国外交部向大韩民国驻华大使馆致意，并谨就大使馆二OO六年七月二十一日驻中大（政）字第2006—415号照会请求引渡 CO 事答复如下：

中方同意韩方引渡 CO 的请求，关于移交被请求引渡人 CO 的时间、地点、方式以及与执行引渡有关的其他事宜，韩方可与中华人民共和国公安部商定。

顺致崇高的敬意。

二OO八年七月 三 日于北京

Korea Times, Sept. 11, 2008

Drug Ring Leader Extradited to Seoul

By Kim Tae-jong
Staff Reporter

Nigerian drug smuggler, CO , 41, is taken to the Seoul Supreme Prosecutors' Office in Seochogu, southern Seoul, Wednesday.
/ Korea Times Photo by Shim Hyun-chul

A Nigerian drug smuggler was extradited to Seoul Wednesday. He allegedly smuggled drugs into Korea from Southeast Asian countries and re-smuggled them to European countries, using Koreans as cariers. The extradition came after a number of Koreans served prison terms in other countries for their involvement in drug smuggling.

Chinese police handed the alleged drug smuggler, CO , 41, over to the Korean government at Incheon International Airport, the Ministry of Justice said.

The extradition was initially designed to help reduce the prison terms of Koreans imprisoned in Britain, the Netherlands, Brazil and Japan, who were accomplices of CO , but due to delays in the extradition process, all had already finished their prison terms and returned to Korea.

The ministry said that the 10 Korean women and two Korean men caught and sent to foreign prisons while delivering drugs, did not know what they were carrying.

The government has long attempted to prove the Koreans were victims of the drug smuggling.

CO , the leader of an international drug ring, and known to speak eight languages including Korean and English, opened a bogus company in Itaewon, Seoul in the early 2000s, according to police.

Passing himself off as an American businessman, he used young Koreans to deliver cocaine and marijuana, which he got from Thailand and Brazil, to drug traffickers in Netherlands, Denmark, Britain and Japan. They simply believed they were getting a free trip to a foreign country in return for the delivery of ``clothing samples."

He has been on the Korean police wanted list since 2002. He fled the country and moved to Europe in 2006 after six of his gang members were arrested and police put him on the list.

He was arrested in Germany in October 2003 and transferred to a prison in Denmark. However, he escaped from the prison in May 2004.

He smuggled himself into Nigeria and started to teach Korean before traveling to China to resume his business. He was arrested there and placed in a prison until now.

The Korean government requested the Chinese government extradite him and the Chinese court accepted the request last October.

Upon successful extradition to Korea, the Narcotics and Organized Crime Investigation Department of the Seoul Central District Prosecutors' Office decided to prosecute *CO* on the basis of violation of the criminal law of Korea.[104]

Legal Assistance from Denmark and Other Countries

In its efforts to prosecute *CO* and secure material evidence, the Korean Prosecution Service then requested legal assistance for obtaining investigation records and court decisions from concerned

---

104 ***Act on the Aggravated Punishment of Specific Crimes***

Article 11 (Aggravated Punishment of Narcotic Offender, etc.)

(1) Any person who commits a crime as prescribed in Article 58 (1) 1 through 4, 6 and 7 of the Act on the Control of Narcotics, etc. (excluding the crime of trading, transferring, receiving, or delivering the relevant substances or the crime of holding or possessing the relevant substances for trade, or assistance in trade, or transfer or receipt) or makes an attempt to commit such a crime shall be punished by imprisonment for life or not less than ten years.

Act on the Control of Narcotics

Article 58 (Penal Provisions)

(1) Any person who falls under any of the following subparagraphs shall be punished by imprisonment for life or for not less than five years:

1. A person who imports or exports, manufactures, trades, or assists in the trade of, narcotics, or who holds or possesses narcotics for import or export, manufacture, trade, or assistance in trade, in violation of subparagraphs 2 through 4 of Article 3, or Article 4 (1), 18 (1) or 21 (1);

Article 4 (Prohibition of Handling Narcotics, etc. by Unauthorized Persons)

(1) No person other than a person authorized to handle narcotics, etc. shall be allowed to carry, possess, use, transport, control, import, export (limited to psychotropic drugs), manufacture, prepare, dose, trade, assist in trade of, give or receive, or deliver narcotics or psychotropic drugs: to cultivate, carry, possess, give or receive, transport, provide custody for, or use marijuana; to issue prescriptions for narcotics or psychotropic drugs; or to manufacture the non-addictive narcotic substance: Provided, that the same shall not apply to any of the following cases: *<Amended by Act No. 8852, Feb. 29, 2008; Act No. 9932, Jan. 18, 2010>*

countries including Denmark, France, Spain, Argentina, Netherland, and Peru. From September of 2003 to February of 2007, eleven Korean drug carriers who worked for *CO* were brought to trial for their roles in trafficking 57kg of cocaine. If evidence were to be obtained from these countries, the Korean Prosecution Service felt that it would doubtlessly lead to a successful prosecution of *CO* in Korea.

Among the above-mentioned countries, all but France accepted Korea's request for legal assistance. Below are the acceptance letters that were received from Denmark, Spain, and Peru.

Acceptance of the Mutual Legal Request by Denmark (1)

JUSTITSMINISTERIET

Ministry of Justice
Civil and Police Department

Korean Supreme Prosecutor's Office

Date:
Office: International Division
Contact: Caroline Maibohm Lyck
Our ref.: 2008-3400-2485
Doc.: CLY40191

Your reference: DK38.1108

Dear Madam/Sir,

By letter of 5 November 2008 the Korean authorities requested the assistance of the Danish authorities for the purpose of executing a letter rogatory concerning Woo Jin Yoon.

The letter rogatory is hereby returned.

Please find enclosed the information provided by the Central and West Jutland Police.

Yours faithfully,

Acceptance of the Mutual Legal Request by Denmark (2)

RIGSPOLITIET
AFDELING A - NEC
Rejseholdet
Polititorvet 14 – 1780 København V
Tlf. 33 14 88 88 – Telefax 33 32 27 71
Email: nec@politi.dk

Journalnr. 4400-71282-00001-03, m.fl.	
Forhold	Bilag A-0-0-0-0

KOPI

p.t. kriminalpolitiet i Silkeborg
onsdag d. 14. juli 2004

RAPPORT

Vedrørende: sagen mod Frank Chinedu Obioha, Per Dyrby Ludvigsen, Woo Jin Yoon, So Joong Yoon, Hwan See Le, der alle sigtes for overtrædelse af straffelovens § 191.

Angående: **Resumé**

Sagen er grupperet i bilag som følger:
A: anmeldelse
B: anholdelse/ransagning
C: afhøringer (sigtede/vidner)
D: anmodninger til retten
E: retsbøger
F: efterforskning
G: retsanmodninger
H: koster
I: Tekniske undersøgelser / gerningsstedet
L: andre erklæringer
N: Regnskaber / E&S
O: observation
P: indgreb i meddelelseshemmeligheden
T: advokatskrivelser
V: skrivelser til og fra andre.

Forklaring til bilagering:
1. tal efter 1. bogstav i bilagene tilknytter sig en person.
Hvor 1 er anført som første tal vedrører bilaget mere en 1 person.
Det kan nævnes, at de i sagen sigtede, har følgende nummer efter bogstav:

Woo Jin Yoon:	**2**
Frank Chinedu Obioha:	**3**
Per Dyrby Ludvigsen:	**4**
So Joong Yoon:	**5**
Hwan Se Lee:	**16**

Eks. Bilag C-2-3 læses som: C= afhøring, 2= Woo Jin Yoon & 3 = 3. bilag
Eks. Bilag F-1-8 læses som: F = efterforskning, 1= flere personer & 8 = 8. bilag.

./. Bilagsfortegnelse og personoversigt vedlægges.

Indledning:

Acceptance of the Mutual Legal Request by Spain

MINISTERIO DE ASUNTOS EXTERIORES Y DE COOPERACIÓN

SECRETARIA GENERAL DE ASUNTOS CONSULARES Y MIGRATORIOS

DIRECCIÓN GENERAL DE ASUNTOS Y ASISTENCIA CONSULARES

Núm.

Ref. 110603-CR-08

NOTA VERBAL

El Ministerio de Asuntos Exteriores y de Cooperación saluda atentamente a la Embajada de Corea en esta capital y, con referencia a su Nota Verbal núm. MSP/08/24, de 12.11.08, adjunto le remite documentación judicial, procedente del Ministerio de Justicia, relativa a OBIOHA FRANK CHINDEU, SUH JIN YOUNG Y OTROS, con diligencias practicadas por la Fiscalía Antidroga.

El Ministerio de Asuntos Exteriores y de Cooperación reitera a la Embajada de Corea el testimonio de su alta consideración.

Madrid, 20 de mayo de 2009

AUDIENCIA PROVINCIAL DE MADRID
Sección nº 23
AVDA. SANTIAGO DE COMPOSTELA, N 96
Tfno.: 91 493 4645/6/4722 Fax: 91 - 493 46 39

09921 OFICIO LIBRE

Número de Identificación Único: 28000 2 7096275 /2006
Ejecutoria : 111 /2007
Rollo : 59 /2006
Órgano Procedencia: JDO. INSTRUCCION N. 18 de MADRID
Proc. Origen: SUMARIO (PROC.ORDINARIO) nº 11 /2006
Contra: JIN YOUNG SEU
Procurador/a: MARIA TERESA MARCOS MORENO
Abogado/a: MA DE LAS MERCEDES CARRE?O ARNAL

En virtud de lo acordado en resolución de esta fecha en la Ejecutoria arriba indicada, y dando cumplimiento a lo solicitado en su oficio de fecha 20/02/2009, adjunto remito testimonio de los particulares interesados a fin de que surta los efectos oportunos en su Comisión Rogatoria nº 139/2008.

En MADRID , a dieciseis de marzo de dos mil nueve

LA SECRETARIA.

FISCALIA ESPECIAL ANTIDROGA.
AUDIENCIA NACIONAL.
Calle García Gutiérrez s/n. 28004 MADRID.

Acceptance of the Mutual Legal Request by Peru

D DE RELACIONES
TERIORES
8084
NOV 2009
10.10
ón General de
tos Legales

"Año de la Unión Nacional frente a la Crisis Externa"

2009 NOV 4 PM 4 00

Ministerio Público

RECIBIDO
MESA DE PARTES

OFICIO N° 3948-2009-MP-FN-UCJIE

Lima, 03 NOV. 2009

Señora Embajadora
BERTHA VEGA PEREZ
Directora General de Asuntos Legales
Ministerio de Relaciones Exteriores
Presente.-

Ref: OF.RE (DGL) N° 4-3-A/932
27/10/2008

Tengo el agrado de dirigirme a usted a fin de remitirle en fojas 154, el Oficio N° 11662-2009-P-CSJCL/PJ, cursado por el presidente de la Corte Superior del Callao, por el que remite la solicitud de Asistencia Judicial librada por el Fiscal de la Oficina de la Fiscalía del Distrito Central de Seúl – Corea del Sur, relativa a la Investigación seguida contra **CHOI KWANGSU, LEE SEONJOO** y **otro**, por delito de Tráfico Ilícito de Drogas, en agravio del Estado.

En tal sentido, se servirá tener a bien transmitir con **CARÁCTER DE URGENTE**, la aludida asistencia judicial a las autoridades competentes de Corea del Sur, para los fines pertinentes.

Es propicia la oportunidad para expresar los sentimientos de mi deferencia.

Atentamente,

CECILIA HINOJOSA CUBA
Fiscal Adjunta Suprema Titular
Jefe de la Unidad de Cooperación Judicial Internacional y Extradiciones

AJ 467-2008
Reg. N° 24589
SH/YC

MESA DE PARTES
RECIBIDO
CODIGO 4-3 1797
Trámite a cargo de
DGL – 4 NOV. 2009
Copias para información
1
2
Observaciones

Ministerio Público — *Defensor de la Legalidad*

Justice Administered

As evidence were successfully obtained for the trial of *CO*, the Supreme Court of Korea eventually confirmed the decision by the district and appellate courts and sentenced *CO* to life in prison and a fine of 100 million Korean won (USD 80,000).

Successful Case of Both Extradition and Legal Assistance

The most fundamental legal mechanisms for international cooperation in criminal matters are extradition and mutual legal assistance, as described before.[105] It is noteworthy in this case that both of these mechanisms were fully utilized to successfully convict *CO*.

Furthermore, even though China was not a concerned party with regards to the actual crime, it still accepted the request for extradition of *CO* to Korea. This instance of extraditing the fugitive from another country that had no nexus with the crime or nationality of either the suspect or the victim served as a positive example in the field of extradition and paved the way for a broader implementation of mutual cooperation in criminal matters.

Most importantly, *Nigerian Drug Dealer Case* illustrates the current state of how international crimes operate and how its resulting

105 Explained in Section I. *Traditional Framework of International Cooperation.*

Korea Herald, March 30, 2010

Nigerian drug trafficker sentenced to life in prison

2010-03-30

The Supreme Court on Wednesday sentenced a Nigerian drug dealer, who used South Korean travelers to transport banned substances, to life in prison and a fine of 100 million won ($80,000), according to Yonhap News.

CO , 42, was convicted last year of using South Koreans -- mostly young women -- as mules to traffick cocaine and marijuana.

He fled to China with a forged passport after South Korean prosecutors launched an investigation in 2002, but was arrested at a German airport the following year and then transferred to Denmark. He managed to escape from a Danish prison while awaiting trial in 2004, and resurfaced in China in 2007. Seoul had him extradited from Beijing last year.

A district court and an appellate court convicted him of drug trafficking and gave life imprisonment.

impacts are far-reaching, beyond borders. Since crimes are crossing borders, it has now become inevitable that measures to counteract these crimes involve a different perspective than before. As displayed by the relentless pursuit of *CO* by the Korean authorities, the key to a successful punishment would lie in the collaborative efforts and multilateral cooperation between all nations.

Case Timetable

Date	Event
1999. 6. 30	A bogus company named 'Fechinco Korea' was set up in Seoul, Korea as a middle ground for drug smuggling.
2000 ~	*CO* started to entice Korean women into becoming drug carriers.
2002. 5. 17	By utilizing Park (Korean female) as a drug carrier, *CO* smuggled 33.12kg of cocaine into Korea from the U.K., Brazil, and the Netherlands.
2002. 6. 30	*CO* fled to Germany with a forged passport.
2003. 10. 21	*CO* was arrested by the Interpol at the Frankfurt Airport in Germany.
2003. 11. 21	1st extradition request: Korea requested extradition of *CO* from Germany.
2004. 2. 17	Extradition from Germany to Denmark. (Denmark requested extradition of *CO* on Jan 2004)
2004. 5. 21	2nd extradition request: Korea requested extradition of *CO* from Denmark.
2004. 5. 28	*CO* escaped from Aarhus detention center in Denmark, while awaiting trial.
2005. 4	*CO* fled to China with a forged passport.
2006. 7. 10	3rd extradition request: Korea requested extradition of *CO* from China.
2007. 2	*CO* was captured by the Ministry of Public Security of China.
2007. 10	The High Court of Liaoning, China approved extradition request by Korea.
2008. 6	Final approval by the Chinese Foreign Ministry to extradite *CO*.
2008. 9. 11	*CO* returned to Korea via Korean Air.

2008. 9. 23	*CO* was prosecuted for violation of Act of Aggravated Punishment, etc. of Specific Crimes Article 11 and Act on the Control of Narcotics, etc. Article 4 and 58.
2008. 11. 8	Mutual legal assistance provided by Denmark for court records of Korean drug carriers who worked under *CO* and who were tried in the respective countries, and also provided by Spain, Argentina, Netherland and Peru.
2009. 1	*CO* was sentenced to life imprisonment and a fine of 100 million Korean won (USD 80,000) by the district and appellate courts in Korea.
2009. 7	The Supreme Court of Korea confirmed his conviction and sentence.

5. *Seorae* French Village Infanticide Case

Summary of the Case

Two infant corpses were found in a refrigerator at the residence of a French national who was living in Korea. After conducting DNA testing of the infants, the Korean authorities confirmed that the infants were children of *VC*. Since the mother *VC* had already returned to France, jurisdictional disputes occurred between the two countries. After a series of official and unofficial discussions, both countries agreed to put the case on trial in a French court, using evidences provided by the Korean authorities. As a result of successful legal cooperation, *VC* was convicted of infanticide in the French court.

Frozen Babies Were Found in a Refrigerator

VC's husband had worked as an engineer at the Seoul branch of xxxx Systems in Korea since August 1, 2002. Thereafter, his wife, *VC*, and two sons moved to Korea on August 20, 2002. They began to

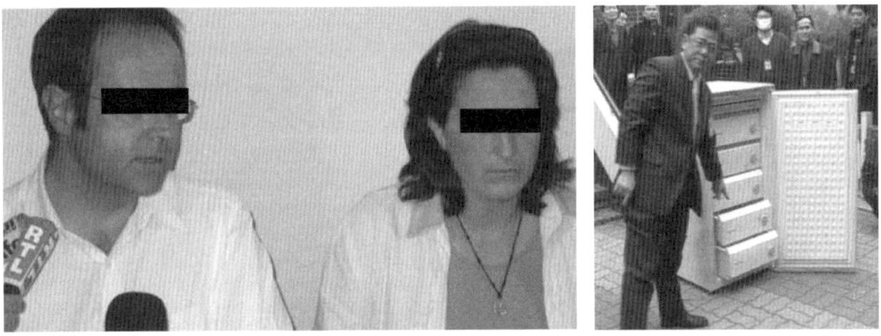

VC and her husband during a press conference in Tours, France in August 22, 2006 (left); The freezer where the babies were found (right)

reside in the *Seorae* Village of Seoul, an area of concentrated French population.

While the *VC* family was spending their vacation in Touraine, France, from June 29, 2006, *VC*'s husband, *JC* returned to Korea on July 18 due to work-related matters. Upon his arrival, he checked his security system and found no signs or record of a break-in. At 11 am, July 23, he received a package of frozen mackerel while he was alone in his house.

After receiving the package, he headed to the refrigerator which was located in the utility room and opened the fourth shelf in the freezer. Inside the black & white plastic bag which was placed in the shelf, he found a newborn baby wrapped around in a towel. In the fifth shelf in the freezer, he found another infant contained in a black plastic bag. He immediately called his co-worker and asked him to report the frozen babies to the police.

Flow Chart of the Case Proceedings

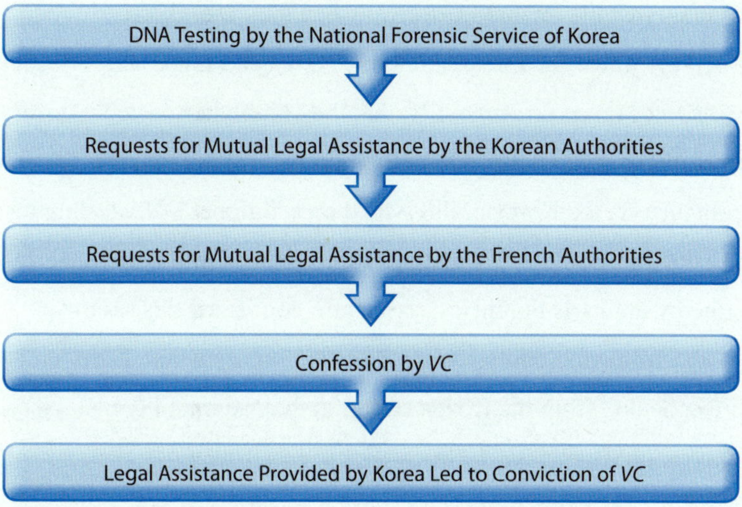

Investigation & DNA Testing Initiated by Korea

VC's husband testified to the police that he knew nothing about the babies and did not point out any possible suspects related to this incident. The Korean National Police Agency collected evidence in the house and took all measures necessary for the investigation. *VC*'s husband departed for France without any restriction on July 26.

As the case proceeded, the police could not leave out the possibility of *VC*'s husband being connected to the incident. He was the first person to discover the babies and the incident took place at his residence. With his consent, the National Forensic Service (NFS) of Korea conducted DNA testing of the babies and reported on July 28 that, the infants had genes identical to those of *VC*'s husband.

According to the autopsy and DNA testing report by the Korean NFS, it seemed that the infants were alive when they were born.

In the midst of investigations by Korea & France, the *VC* couple testified in France on August 10 that they highly suspected conspiracy and strongly denied allegations that the babies were theirs. However, on August 17, the Korean NFS issued an additional DNA testing result and confirmed that *VC* was the mother of the infants.[106] The DNA testing by the Paris Forensic Service also confirmed this result.

The following photos below show the scenes where DNA samples were collected from the frozen babies at the National Forensic Service of Korea, on August 25, 2006.

Collection of DNA samples by Korean NFS

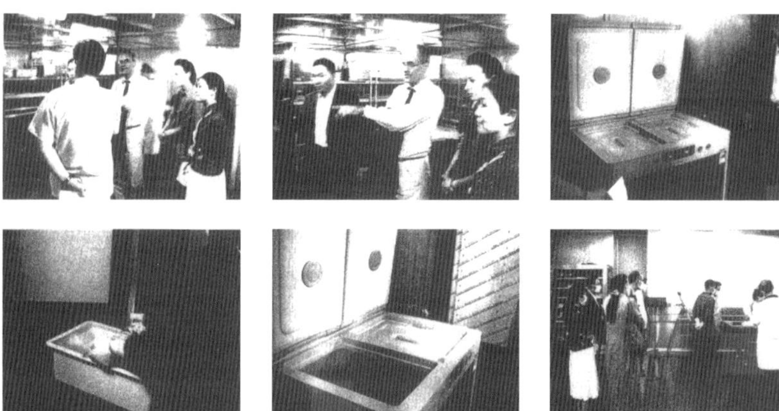

106 *VC* had a uterus removal surgery on December 13, 2003, and the DNA testing samples were retrieved from the place of surgery, Seoul St. Mary's Hospital.

Confirmation that the sampling was conducted with witnesses in attendance

CONFIRMATION

In 25th August(today), resampling for the biological(genetic) evaluation of the already autopsied abandoned babies(autopsy date : 24th July 2006, registration number of N. I. S. I : 2006-45434, 2006-45435) is performed with attendance of person from Bang-Bae police, person from french embassy. These samples was sealed under certification of attendance and will be kept in deep-freezer in N. I. S. I. till request of Korea prosecutor's office.

Caution : If these sealed samples have to be transported from nation to nation, these samples have to be refrigerated and delivered within 48hrs(as fast as possible) to the foreign examiner directly. For this, the cooperation of the related person or institute of the both nations will be needed.

25th Aug. 2006

National Institute of Scientific Investigation Seoul, Korea

French Embassy, Seoul, Korea

Dual Criminal Jurisdiction between Korea and France

Immediately after the investigation began, the Korean authorities submitted an informal request of mutual legal assistance to the French Authorities as they needed to deliver the summons and interrogate the *VC* couple who were staying in France.

However, the French authorities refused the requests made by the Korean authorities and officially denied the compulsory return of the *VC* couple to Korea. On August 2, the French Prosecution Service initiated its own investigation. The decision by the French authorities to refuse the requests made by the Korean authorities was not a surprise, because traditionally most states have been of the position that extraditing their own national is not possible.

On the other hand, the French authorities requested mutual legal assistance to the Korean authorities on August 7. This request was based on the *Treaty on Mutual Assistance in Criminal Matters between the Government of the Republic of Korea and the Government of the French Republic*.[107]

It is worth noting that both Korea and France had criminal jurisdiction over the case. Since the crime took place on Korean territory, Korea had criminal jurisdiction. France also had jurisdiction because both of the suspects and victims were French citizens. Deciding which country should exercise jurisdiction involved the following considerations:

(1) Resolving questions of facts and proving defendant's criminal culpability;

(2) Guaranteeing due process rights for defendants;

(3) Determining which government has more interest in bringing justice; and

(4) Ensuring that the defendants receive punishment fitting their crime of infanticide.

107 Signed in March 2, 1995 and entered into force in March 8, 1997.

Taking the above factors into account, Korea decided to convey jurisdiction to France because France already had custody of the defendants and was willing to administer justice. Based on the Treaty on Mutual Legal Assistance, Korea provided all the evidence necessary for proper prosecution.

A Series of Request for Legal Assistance from France

1st MLA request from France to Korea (August 7, 2006)
- All files of the initial Korean investigation
- DNA sample of the infants

↓

MLA request from Korea to France (August 25, 2006)
- Summons delivery to the *VC* couple
- In case of denial, requests for the French authorities to interrogate the *VC* couple in place of the Korean authorities

↓

2nd MLA request from France to Korea (September 5, 2006)
- Preservation of the corpses of the babies
- Postponement of the funeral proceedings

↓

3rd MLA request from France to Korea (October 27, 2006)
- Remaining investigation files from Korean authorities
- Credibility check on the interrogation of the *VC* couple
- Files on *VC* giving birth to the babies
- Whether or not people were aware of *VC*'s pregnancy

After a series of MLA requests by the French authorities, the French Prosecution Service made a provisional arrest of the *VC* couple

Letter from France to Korea on August 18, 2006

COUR D'APPEL D'ORLEANS
TRIBUNAL DE GRANDE INSTANCE DE TOURS
Place Jean-Jaurès - 37032 TOURS CEDEX - Tél. : 02.47.60.26.60
PARQUET

Parquet général d'Orléans
21 AOUT 2006

TOURS, le 18 août 2006

LE PROCUREUR DE LA REPUBLIQUE
à

Toutes autorités judiciaires compétentes
de la République de COREE DU SUD

S/C Madame le Procureur Général
Près la Cour d'Appel d'ORLEANS

Monsieur le Garde des Sceaux
Ministre de la Justice

REF. : Parquet n° 06/7210 - MC/DP

Vu la convention d'entraide judiciaire franco-coréenne du 2 mars 1995

Pour faire suite et en complément de sa précédente demande du 9 août 2006 le procureur de la république soussigné vous serait très obligé de bien vouloir faire assurer la conservation des deux corps des nouveaux-nés et de surseoir à toutes opérations funéraires afin de permettre la réalisation des expertises médico-légales qui seront jugées utiles ou demandées par les parties.

Le Procureur soussigné remercie les autorités de la République de Corée du Sud de leur collaboration et les assure de sa très haute considération.

LE PROCUREUR DE LA REPUBLIQUE,

Michel CRUZ, Procureur de la République Adjoint

on October 10.

Confession by *VC* in French Court

At first, the *VC* couple strongly denied that they were the parents of the frozen babies. However, on October 11, *VC* confessed to the French authorities that she had suffocated the babies after giving birth to them in her bathtub. She had concealed her pregnancies from her husband, who was often away on business, and also from her neighbors. *VC* concealed her pregnancies well enough that even her sister-in-law who was a medical doctor did not notice her changes. Classmates at her yoga class were also unable to notice her physical differences.

According to her confession, she gave birth to the babies in the mornings of October 2002 and December 2003, while her husband was at work and her two children had gone to school. After hearing the babies cry, she suffocated them to death. She then cleaned the bathtub and took a nap. She explained that she used similar methods of births and killings for both babies.

She also confessed that she had killed another child she had given birth to in July 1999, while living in France. She said that she disposed the body of the first child by burning it in the fireplace of her home.

Legal Assistance by Korea Led to Conviction of *VC*

On October 12, 2006, *VC* was imprisoned in the Orleans prison and *VC*'s husband was held under judicial control. In its efforts to meet the request for MLA from France and proceed the investigation, the Korean authorities provided legal assistance to the French officers who were dispatched to Korea in February of 2007.

In accordance with the *Treaty on Mutual Assistance on Criminal Matters between Korea and France*, the French authorities wanted to procure corroborating evidence to prove *VC*'s confession and to investigate whether or not *VC*'s husband participated in or knew about the killings of the babies.

The letter on the next page is from the Director of International Criminal Affairs, Ministry of Justice in Korea, accepting the visit of French officers with regards to the investigation in Korea.[108]

With the successful legal assistance from the Korean authorities, the French court, on June 19, 2009, eventually convicted *VC* of murdering three of her newborn children and sentenced her to eight years.[109]

---

108 According to the letter, the French officers were originally scheduled to visit Korea in January, but their business in France delayed their schedule until February.

109 Pregnancy Denial;

In France, murder charges carry a maximum penalty of life in prison but the prosecutor had recommended that *VC* be given a 10-year prison sentence. As she was ultimately sentenced to eight years in prison, she will only serve five years of her sentence because she had been in custody for three years during the investigation.

During the trial, in the western city of Tours, psychiatrists testified that *VC* suffered from a psychological condition known as "pregnancy denial", and family members pleaded

The Letter Accepting the Visit of French Officers Regarding Investigation in Korea, December 26, 2006

MINISTRY OF JUSTICE REPUBLIC OF KOREA

MINISTRY OF JUSTICE

1 Jungang-dong, Gwacheon, 427-720, Republic of Korea

December 26, 2006

Samuel Lainé
Chef de Section
Direction des Affaires Criminelles et des Grâces
Ministère de la Justice
République Française

Dear Mr. Samuel Lainé

I would like to welcome the visit of the French officers, who are handling the investigation of the Frozen babies case, which will be made to Korea from January 11 to January 26, 2007.

The Korean Ministry of Justice permits the presence of the French investigative officers during the investigative procedure related to the frozen babies case based on the Treaty on the Mutual Legal Assistance in Criminal Matters between the Republic of Korea and the Republic of France and the Act on the International Legal Assistance in Criminal Matters of the Republic of Korea, and will provide all the possible assistance.

For your information, Korean Minister of Justice, H.E. KIM Sung-Ho, plans to visit the French Ministry of Justice and discuss measures to strengthen the cooperation between the Korean Ministry of Justice and the French Ministry of Justice and seek a collaborative way regarding the mutual legal assistance including the assistance in this case from January 18 to January 19, 2007. As for the visit of the Minister of Justice to France, I would like to ask the French Ministry of Justice to provide the highest considerations and cooperation.

Sincerely yours,

HWANG, Cheol-kyu
Director
International Criminal Affairs Division
Ministry of Justice
Republic of Korea

Collaborative Effort to Bring Justice

It is praiseworthy that the full range of legal assistance was provided by the Korean authorities to successfully convict *VC* in France. Not only were all investigative files forwarded to France, but the French authorities also visited Korea to further investigate the case. This demonstrated an ideal model for very close collaborative effort for mutual cooperation in criminal justice.

In addition, the Korean authorities demonstrated their excellence in the field of DNA testing as they successfully verified the parents of the babies. With evidentiary basis becoming more and more crucial in the investigation process, the highest level of scientific technique is needed more than ever before. Hopefully, this case will play an leading role in promoting international cooperation in criminal investigation that requires this level of scientific technique.

---

for clemency on her behalf. Her husband praised the relatively light sentence, which he said "will allow us to rebuild, to make out the light at the end of the tunnel". He believed his wife had "big problems" and that "It's clear that *VC*'s actions were absolutely not calculated. For me, she's ill".

In the testimony two days before the sentence, *VC* had confessed to the triple infanticide. "I killed my children," she said between sobs. She added that "absurd" as it may sound, "I was conscious of being pregnant, but not of being pregnant with babies." She said she did not consciously set out to hide the pregnancies. "It was my body that blocked the pregnancies." she said. "No relationship with the babies developed."

Case Timetable

Date	Event
2006. 7. 23	- Two corpses of frozen infants were found in a refrigerator in their house. - Korean police collected evidence and initiates an investigation.
2006. 7. 28	National Forensic Service of Korea reported that the babies had identical genes with *JC* according to the DNA testing.
2006. 8. 1	- Korea charged *JC* and *VC* with infanticide and corpse abandonment. - Korea subpoenaed the suspects and requests France for assistance in locating and interviewing the suspects.
2006. 8. 2	- Tours Prosecution Service in France initiated investigation. - French government denied the repatriation of the *VC* couple to Korea.
2006. 8. 7	1st MLA request from France to Korea. - All files of the initial Korean investigation. - DNA sample of the infants.
2006. 8. 17	National Forensic Service of Korea reported that *VC* was the mother of the infants according to the DNA testing.
2006. 8. 25	MLA request from Korea to France. - Summons delivery to the *VC* couple. - In case of denial, requests for the French authorities to interrogate the *VC* couple in place of the Korean authorities.
2006. 9. 5	2nd MLA request from France to Korea. - Preservation of the corpses of the babies. - Postponement of the funeral proceedings.
2006. 10. 11	*VC* confessed.
2006. 10. 12	*VC* was imprisoned and *JC* was held under judicial control, both in France.
2006. 10. 27	3rd MLA request from France to Korea. - Remaining investigation files from Korean authorities. - Credibility check on the interrogation of the *VC* couple.

2007. 2. 12 ~ 2. 22	French officers were dispatched to Korea to procure corroborating evidence and to advance the investigation.
2009. 6. 19	French court convicted *VC* of murdering three of her newborn baby and sentences her to eight years in prison. - *JC* was not charged with complicity in the lower court.

IV. NEW INITIATIVES ON INTERNATIONAL COOPERATION

1. Direct Contact and Speedy Response

Transformation of Ways to Cooperate

As stated in the foreword, traditionally, the law enforcement of each nation used to limit the scope of its activities to its own jurisdiction. The concept of jurisdiction is self-imposed and very strict based on the theory of sovereignty. Crime, however, is not subject to such concept of jurisdiction. Criminals tend to commit crimes regardless of jurisdiction. Nowadays, national borderlines can be easily crossed. But law enforcement agencies are confined within the borderlines and the concept of national jurisdiction.

In the *English Instructor Murder Case*, we saw how extradition efforts failed between the U. S. and Korea due to the fact that there was no extradition treaty between the two countries at the time of the request and no further cooperation was even attempted. Furthermore, due to the lack of communication, Korea was unaware that there was upcoming legislation in the U.S. that would give the U.S. jurisdiction over the *English Instructor Murder Case*. By the time the legislation had passed, Korea had already destroyed the evidence, and the criminal was able to escape prosecution for charges of murder.

On the other hand, we saw a successful effort of mutual legal assistance in the *Fled Rapist Case* between the U.S. and Korea by way of liaison, through the role of the legal attaché of the Korean Embassy. Besides its success in bringing justice, many lessons were learned as well. Even though the criminal was ultimately punished in Korea, the cooperation process for prosecution and trial was too lengthy and complicated. A simple request for a witness testimony had to go through multiple channels until a solution was found. And even then, the entire process required many formalities and took years to complete.

Thus, we should not fixate on the concept of jurisdiction any longer and should look for effective ways to overcome the limits of jurisdiction and go beyond the sovereignty concept embedded in the diplomatic channels through close cooperation between law enforcement agencies.

Universal jurisdiction on transnational crime could be the ultimate future goal of law enforcement agencies in their fight against transnational crime. However, that has a long way to go. Currently, universal jurisdiction is only narrowly recognized for serious and specific areas of crime such as genocide.[110] In addition, the jurisdiction

110 Charlotte Ku, The Dynamics of International Law at 91. Over the past sixty years, there has not been much change in jurisdiction provisions of genocide. The war crimes tribunals for the former Yugoslavia and Rwanda both include provisions for concurrent jurisdiction between national courts and the tribunals, but international courts were given primacy. The International Criminal Court defers prosecution to states that have jurisdiction, but allows the ICC to take action only when such states are "unwilling or unable genuinely to carry

of the International Tribunal, such as the International Criminal Court, is complementary to that exercised by national authorities.[111] The concept of universal jurisdiction conflicts with the theory of sovereignty.

Each nation is sovereign, and the international society should respect this. The sovereignty of each country makes its own territorial jurisdiction for investigation and prosecution of crimes. The only way to counteract transnational crime while respecting the sovereignty of each State[112] is cooperation between the law enforcement agencies of each country.

As you can see, the traditional model of cooperation is not enough to counteract the current trends of transnational crime. The traditional methods of cooperation are too time-consuming and there are too many diplomatic formalities. The process of cooperation is ineffective and inefficient. It does not catch up with the speedy way of life in the globalized era. We need to transform methods of international cooperation.

Pursuing an Innovative Model of Cooperation

To cope with transnational crimes, we are looking for a new initiative on international cooperation in criminal justice. What is

---

out the investigation or prosecution."

111 *Id.* at 33.

112 Prosecutors must counteract transnational crimes, but respect the sovereignty of their country.

needed in this speedy and internationalized world is 'direct contact' between law enforcement agencies and 'speedy response' to their requests.

In fact, this is the development that has been emerging in both extradition and mutual legal assistance throughout the world. The overall trend for extradition and mutual legal assistance has been to step away from the traditional means that were mostly slow, bilateral, and limited in scope. Not only are there more multilateral treaties with less limitations and grounds for denial, there is also a distinct trend toward less rigid procedural requirements, including direct communications and simplified procedures.[113] This is especially obvious in matters of mutual legal assistance. Traditional MLA treaties required that requests be sent through diplomatic channels or through central authorities, but more recent treaties are allowing the use of direct contacts.[114]

This trend is not surprising since informal channels of cooperation is a more effective means of cooperation in many cases because of all the difficulties that formal means of cooperation present.[115] There are various channels that can be used to obtain informal assistance and nothing prevents relevant authorities from using direct contact and informal networks.

For example, a Memorandum of Understanding on Mutual Cooperation (MOU) between each country's prosecution services or

---

113 Joutsen, *supra* at 391-393.

114 *Id.* at 392.

115 U4 Anti-Corruption Resource Center, Mutual Legal Assistance Treaties and Money Laundering, Part 2.

between the prosecution service and other relevant authorities is often used to facilitate communication between the law enforcement agents. It is shown in Appendix Sections H-1 and H-2.

Further, INTERPOL, EUROPOL and ASEANPOL have proven to be common, direct, and efficient channels of communication among law enforcement agencies.[116] In Asia, some of the ASEAN countries already have a number of MOUs between member countries to allow the exchange of information between their administrative agencies.

Nevertheless, law enforcement agents are still confined to their own territory when handling criminal activities. But, criminals easily cross the borderline of the territory for their crimes. The best way to overcome this basic problem is to establish a new cooperation system to lower the barriers of sovereignty. We can lower the fence and make a side door of friendship with neighbors. That is the main concept of new initiatives on international cooperation in criminal justice.

'Direct Contact and Speedy Response' should be the principle of the new initiative on international cooperation in criminal justice. Under this principle, we can create a new mechanism and operation system between law enforcement agencies.

New Mechanism and New Operation

The new framework of international cooperation should be based on 'direct contact and speedy response.' Multilateral treaty

---

116 *Id.*

and regional consolidation is recommended. Multilateral treaties for cooperation in criminal justice must be established in addition to the traditional bilateral approach of cooperation.

UN has made multilateral mechanisms for international cooperation against corruption and organized crimes, such as the *United Nations Convention against Transnational Organized Crime* (*UNTOC*) and the *United Nations Convention against Corruption* (*UNCAC*). But, these treaties only cover serious and specific crimes, not all transnational crimes.

Europe has multilateral treaties on MLA and extradition. Based on mutual recognition, the *European Arrest Warrant* (*EAW*) and the *European Evidence Warrant* (*EEW*) are at work between EU countries. However, regions other than Europe do not have multilateral mechanism for international cooperation.

In recognition of a need for a multilateral cooperation mechanism in the Asia-Pacific, 'The Asia-Pacific Convention for Cooperation in Criminal Justice' was proposed and became the IAP model treaty.[117] It would be a good idea to develop it into a UN regional convention, with continuing efforts of the States in this region.

To establish the multilateral mechanism, regional consolidation is also very important. Cooperation in criminal justice could be supported by strong ties in politics, economy and culture. Europe provides a good example. With the economic and political unification in the region, it was easy to establish a multilateral cooperation system in justice.

The new mechanism of multilateral cooperation, with the principle

117 More details will be discussed in the Section IV, Chapter 2 (IAP Model Treaty).

of direct contact and speedy response, could avoid the unnecessary delay and complexity that accompany the diplomacy and formality under the traditional system. It can also increase the efficiency and effectiveness of international criminal justice.

For the new initiative, we have to make a new operation system of international law enforcement under the principle of 'direct contact and speedy response'. A network between law enforcement agencies and mutual trust between agents is necessary for the operation of the new initiative. In Europe, there are some networks for judicial cooperation, such as *Eurojust, European Judicial Network* in EU. *Ibero-American Legal Assistance Network* (*IberoRed*) is also the network for international cooperation in Latin America.

Networking builds friendship among members and understanding between law enforcement agents from different cultures and legal systems. Direct contact and speedy response could be operated with strong trust between agencies and agents. Trust can be triggered by mutual understanding and friendship.

If prosecution services and prosecutors around the world could have a network and direct contact between them, the cooperation system could work more speedily and smoothly to circumvent the intervening diplomatic channels. This way, resources such as time and manpower can be saved.

There are two representative ways of such networking between prosecutors through which 'direct contact and speed response' can be achieved: *International Association of Prosecutors* (*IAP*) and *World Summit of Prosecutors General, Attorneys General, and Chief Prosecutors*.

The 16th Annual Conference of IAP

The IAP is the one and only worldwide group of prosecutors. Although it has a short history of seventeen years, it has exponentially grown to include more than 146 organizational members,[118] together with 1,500 individual members, representing over 200,000 prosecutors more than 140 jurisdictions all around the world. Every year, the IAP has an annual conference and regional conferences in Europe, Eastern Europe, Northern America, South America, Africa and the Asia & Pacific. At the conferences, prosecutors from different countries have an opportunity to take part in networking, education, and friendship-building. The IAP is a meeting ground where many prosecutors, working-level or high-level, gather together to discuss common issues and share their experiences and expertise.

118 Organisational membership mainly constituted with associations of prosecutors, prosecution services, and organisations established for the promotion of crime prevention measures and the functions connected with the prosecution of crime or an international organisation established by a state or by a prosecution service.

The 4th World Summit of Prosecutors General, Attorneys General and Chief Prosecutors

United Nations E/CN.15/2010/L.7

Economic and Social Council

Distr.: Limited
13 May 2010

Original: English

Commission on Crime Prevention and Criminal Justice
Nineteenth session
Vienna, 17-21 May 2010
Item 4 (d) of the provisional agenda*
Integration and coordination of efforts by the United Nations Office on Drugs and Crime and by Member States in the field of crime prevention and criminal justice: other crime prevention and criminal justice matters

Chile, Republic of Korea and Romania: draft resolution

Hosting of the Fourth World Summit of Attorneys General, Prosecutors General and Chief Prosecutors by the Republic of Korea

The Commission on Crime Prevention and Criminal Justice,

Emphasizing the significance of international cooperation in criminal matters, to which prosecutors can make a major contribution,

Recalling its resolution 18/4 of 24 April 2009, entitled "Fourth World Summit of Attorneys General, Prosecutors General and Chief Prosecutors",

Deeply regretting the devastating natural disaster that struck Chile in February 2010 and that led to the Government of Chile withdrawing its offer to act as host of the Fourth World Summit of Attorneys General, Prosecutors General and Chief Prosecutors,

1. *Takes note* of the conclusions and recommendations of the Third World Summit of Attorneys General, Prosecutors General and Chief Prosecutors, held in Bucharest on 24 and 25 March 2009;[1]

2. *Welcomes* the initiative of the Government of the Republic of Korea to act as host to the Fourth World Summit of Attorneys General, Prosecutors General and Chief Prosecutors, in 2011;

* E/CN.15/2010/1.
[1] E/CN.15/2009/18.

V.10-53705 (E)

Please recycle

E/CN.15/2010/L.7

3. *Requests* the United Nations Office on Drugs and Crime to assist the Government of the Republic of Korea in the preparations for the Fourth World Summit in collaboration with the technical secretariat of the Third World Summit and the International Association of Prosecutors;

4. *Invites* Member States and other donors to provide extrabudgetary contributions, in accordance with the rules and procedures of the United Nations, for assisting in the hosting of the Fourth World Summit.

Prosecutors General who attended the 4th World Summit

The World Summit of Prosecutors General, Attorneys General, and Chief Prosecutors is a chance for the heads of prosecution services of each country to gather together to do the same. The World Summit of Prosecutors General is a unique bi-annual gathering controlled and managed by the UN.

The 4th World Summit was successfully held in Seoul from June 30th to July 1st of 2011. The first three meetings were held in Guatemala, Qatar, and Romania. The Seoul World Summit was attended by representatives of 103 States, making it the largest Summit yet.[119] The Summit itself sought to lay out a more comprehensive approach in dealing with transnational crimes based on close collaboration between the prosecution services of UN countries.

Through such meetings, prosecutors can build networks that

---

119 Also attending the Summit were observers from the United Nations Secretariat, UNODC and other entities and specialized agencies of the UN and intergovernmental and non-governmental organizations.

Plenary Session of the 4th World Summit

will enable them to cooperate directly with each other to achieve international criminal justice in the future.

2. IAP Model Treaty: The Asia-Pacific Convention for Cooperation in Criminal Justice

Background of Proposal

The Asia-Pacific region has experienced impressive economic growth over the last few decades. The removal of trade barriers and the advances in technology and travel have accelerated this growth. Like the rest of the world, these changes were accompanied with the increase of transnational crimes.

For example, it has become easy to conduct transnational financial transactions. Corrupt officials have taken advantage of this situation by siphoning and hiding the proceeds of their crimes abroad, including bribes and embezzled funds. Asia-Pacific countries have seen examples in which corrupt officials transferred millions of dollars of illegal proceeds overseas. Such crimes that cross borders must be fought with instruments that also transcend borders like multilateral treaties.[120]

---

120 Richard Woolcott, *Toward an Asia Pacific Community, The Asialink Essays*, November 2009, at 2.

The rate of growth and change in the region is too great for us to take a passive approach to the emerging challenges. A passive approach entails too high a risk of instability arising within the region. The countries of the region ought to deliberately develop an instrument to meet these challenges, rather than to allow such an instrument to evolve passively, while simply hoping for the best.[121]

For example, as we have seen in many cybercrimes, prompt cooperation is required to cope with various transnational crimes. However, there are weaknesses in this respect in the current system and there is an urgent need to address this problem, especially in responding to the widely spread cybercrimes.

Another example involves how the Asia-Pacific countries also remain vulnerable to money laundering. Given the relatively weak financial and economic monitoring and control systems present in some countries in the region, it is often difficult to follow money trails, which is essential in investigating crimes of this nature. In recent years, the confiscation of proceeds of crimes through MLA has therefore become a focal issue.

However, there is no single mechanism in the Asia-Pacific region with the membership and mandate to comprehensively address the challenges of transnational crimes. Such a tool would be invaluable in managing an increasingly crowded landscape of intra-regional interactions and in ensuring that outward-looking regionalism is sustained as the bedrock of the Asia-Pacific integration.[122]

---

121 *Id.*
122 *Id.*

The only existing region-wide multilateral treaty for cooperation in the area of criminal justice is the *Mutual Legal Assistance in Criminal Matters Treaty for like-minded ASEAN Member Countries*, which has been in effect since 2005.[123] As one can see by the number of requests made and honored in the statistics in Appendix Chart I,[124] there have not been extensive activities under this treaty.[125] Furthermore, this treaty has a limited scope of assistance as it only covers mutual legal assistance.

Some Asia Pacific Countries are also parties to other multilateral treaties,[126] such as UN Conventions[127] and various EU Conventions of MLA and Extradition. However, UN conventions only apply to specific crimes and EU Conventions are uniquely created for EU nations, so they are of little use for the Asia-Pacific region, even though they appear well-structured.

Countries in this region are concluding more and more bilateral

---

123 The groupings and institutions already in place in the Asia-Pacific region are making valuable contributions to the region's stability and prosperity and could become the building blocks of an Asia-Pacific community. ASEAN, a sub-regional organization in the Asia-Pacific, highlights the importance of developing the right mechanisms at the right time. ASEAN played a crucial role in the transformation of Southeast Asia from a region of strategic conflict into one of cooperation and consensus.

124 Recent Statistics on Requests Received and Made under the MLA in Criminal Matters Treaty for like-minded ASEAN Member Countries.

125 More research must be done to determine whether the cause of the low numbers is due to a lack of overall requests, deficiencies in the treaty, or other reasons.

126 Other multilateral treaties in the Asia-Pacific region is the UNCAC, UNTOC, the OECD Convention on Combating Bribery of Foreign Public Officials in International Business Transactions, and the Commonwealth of Independent States Conventions on Legal Assistance and Legal Relationship in Civil, Family, and Civil Matters. Not only are all these treaties focused on fighting specific crimes, they are not instruments unique to the Asia-Pacific region.

127 UNTOC, UNCAC.

treaties with each other, but the number is far from satisfactory and there are a lot of missing links between the countries concerned. In addition, since diplomatic channels are used to establish contact, a great deal of time is wasted when seeking and providing legal assistance, even between contracting States.

Considering the increasing significance of the Asia-Pacific and the growing complexities of the global problems that the region faces, the existing regional mechanisms still lack sufficient mandate and capacity to effectively respond to today's challenges. Confronting the scope of these problems in the Asia-Pacific region, we are in need of an urgent creation of more effective cooperation structures to complement the existing mechanisms. The countries in the region need to establish a multilateral convention reflecting the characteristics of the Asia-Pacific region.

The Asia-Pacific region, which is less compact and more diverse, will have to devise its own structure, based on its own unique historical and cultural background. We have to consider that Asia-Pacific nations differ in many aspects; history, language, ethnics, culture, religion, economy and legal systems. Asia-Pacific countries may take a more flexible approach in formulating its own convention, instead of following the footsteps of the EU,[128] which aims to achieve a comprehensive political and economic integration.

128 As noted in Section II, Europe has now found its own solution—an effective structure and the will to work cooperatively. *Eurojust* provides a good guideline for cooperation but is based on European characteristics.

Constructing the IAP Model Treaty

The Prosecution Service of Korea initiated an extension of the vision of a multilateral mechanism and networking in the Asia-Pacific region. While it could include cooperation in all areas such as economic, security, political and environmental challenges at the governmental level, cooperation in criminal justice was discussed first among prosecutors, to find the most efficient ways to deal with the increase in transnational crimes.

Realizing the importance of sharing such visions, various efforts have been made through the IAP to enhance regional networking in the Asia-Pacific. In 2008, many high-level prosecutors and experts in the Asia-Pacific region gathered at the 5th IAP Regional Conference held in Seoul to discuss thoroughly and comprehensively the ways to promote and strengthen networking among prosecution services in the region. Following the conference, a special meeting of high-level prosecutors was held separately in Busan, Korea.

The heads of prosecution services in Asia-Pacific shared their views on the importance of networking and agreed on the 'Busan Declaration'[129] which promised to strengthen networking for close

---

129 Busan Declaration on Cooperation among High-Level Prosecutors, June 12, 2008

II. We, prosecutors,

1. Concerned about the growing sophistication of transnational organized crime with the advancement of globalization, and recognizing the importance of international cooperation in criminal matters to respond to this challenge,
2. Mindful of the imperative for direct and continuous cooperation among the high level prosecutors to establish an effective and efficient cooperative mechanism for combating transnational crime,

collaboration and the improvement of multilateral cooperation through the IAP.

The fruitful outcomes of the Busan Declaration continued to develop at the Asia-Pacific Regional Forum in the Singapore Annual Conference of IAP in 2008. 'Networking in the Asia-Pacific region' was once again actively discussed at the working-level based on what had been proposed in Korea.

As a first step into a more concrete and wide platform for discussion, the Prosecutor General of Korea, who was also the vice president of the IAP,[130] proposed the 'Asia-Pacific Convention for Cooperation in Criminal Justice' during his opening speech at the 6th IAP Asia-Pacific Regional Conference in Dubai in November 2009. In this proposal, the Korean Prosecutor General highlighted the importance of regional cooperation through IAP network and also the mechanism of 'direct contact and speedy response' between prosecution services based on 'mutual trust' and 'Asian common values.'

III. Declare as follows:

1. We will strengthen and continuously improve a network for constant and close future collaboration.
2. We will endeavor to gradually expand the legal basis for bilateral cooperation by extending, when feasible, the reach of Extradition Treaties and Treaties on Mutual Legal Assistance in Criminal Matters for successful cooperation.
3. We appreciate the international community's efforts to improve multilateral cooperation through the international bodies like IAP, and will strive to increase Asia-Pacific countries' contribution in advancing this collaboration.
4. We will enhance technical cooperation in special fields of crime to efficiently respond to transnational crimes by enhancing the capacity of each country.
5. We will continuously seek inclusive cooperation methods on the basis of understanding and respecting the different legal systems of each country.

130 Author of this book, 37th Prosecutor General of Korea.

Korea's proposal on the 'Asia-Pacific Convention for Cooperation in Criminal Justice' launched a process of dialogue between prosecutors on collectively designing an overarching and effective regional architecture for multilateral cooperation in Asia-Pacific. In order to realize the Dubai proposal, it was agreed that the draft of the Convention would be first developed as an IAP model treaty within the IAP business plan at the 2010 IAP Executive Committee Meeting in Prague.[131]

The Korean Prosecution Service then developed an initial draft and first introduced it during the Hague Annual Conference of IAP in 2010. After incorporating the opinions gathered in Hague, the Initial Draft was distributed to more than twenty-five Asia-Pacific prosecution services for their review and to gather opinions.[132] After incorporating the opinions gathered from the prosecution services in Asia-Pacific, the Korean Prosecution Service prepared a revised draft and introduced it again at the Vienna Executive Committee Meeting of IAP in March 2011. Following the Meeting, the draft of the model treaty was presented at the High-Level Meeting at the 2011 Asia-Pacific Regional Conference of IAP in Indonesia.[133]

---

131 The IAP provided the most suitable platform to build a model treaty for regional cooperation, which also corresponds to the objective of the IAP.

132 In January of 2011, Korea's Prosecutor General visited China and met with the Chinese Procurator-General and agreed to carry forward the Model Treaty as a joint cooperative work with Prosecution Services in China & Korea.

133 Jakarta Declaration, March 18, 2011
III. Declares as follows:
...
2. We acknowledge the laudable efforts of IAP, Korea, and China to advance regional cooperation by development of an IAP Model Treaty.
3. We will endeavor to actively contribute to the continued development of such

After reviewing and reflecting opinions from the Asia-Pacific countries, the Korean Prosecution Service subsequently drew up the final draft and distributed it to the prosecution services in Asia-Pacific. At the 2011 Seoul Annual Conference, the IAP presented the final draft as the IAP Model Treaty for the 'Asia-Pacific Convention for Cooperation in Criminal Justice'. The IAP Model Treaty,[134] as a possible means for strengthening regional cooperation in criminal matters, was presented and discussed at the Asia-Pacific Regional Summit during the World Summit of Prosecutors General[135] held immediately following the IAP Annual Conference.

Main Features of the IAP Model Treaty

The IAP Model Treaty proposes a multilateral and comprehensive treaty between the Asia-Pacific countries. It aims to benefit the entire region by promoting timely and efficient cooperation. 'Direct contact and speedy response' is the core principle of the Model Treaty. Much wasted time and manpower could be saved by circumventing the

---

framework for regional cooperation, which will be further discussed at the 2011 IAP Annual Conference and World Summit of Prosecutors General in Seoul.

134 The full text of the Model Treaty is provided in Appendix Section G.

135 Seoul Declaration on New Initiatives of the Prosecution Service – Fair and Just Society, July 1, 2011

18. We encourage efforts to strengthen operational cooperation among prosecution authorities at the regional level, including through effective networking and information exchange. In this regard, we further welcome the initiative of the Korean Prosecution Service to develop for the Asia-Pacific region an IAP Model Treaty for the Asia-Pacific Convention on cooperation in Criminal Justice.

intervening diplomatic channels.

The Model Treaty is a comprehensive cooperation mechanism covering all the necessary issues including extradition, mutual legal assistance, transfer of sentenced persons, asset recovery, and technical assistance. We have included all methods of cooperation that any of the parties could do, because this is an illustrative model treaty.

A recent report by the working group on countering money laundering and promoting international legal cooperation[136] indicates that although most countries have laws in place and have entered into bilateral and multilateral treaties, legal cooperation still faces major implementation challenges, such as insufficient law enforcement cooperation at the interregional level, lack of training on effective means of making or granting cooperation requests, and remaining difficulties relating to differences among legal systems, and procedural delays and language problems.[137]

A draft of the convention has been provided in the Appendix. The following sections elaborate on the main contents of the Model Treaty.

General Clauses

As for the scope of application, the Model Treaty shall apply to transnational crimes (Article 2). An offence is defined as transnational if it involves more than two countries and if there is a definable link between them. 'Transnational' is defined quite broadly, especially in

---

136 It is set up within the framework of UNODC's Commission on Narcotic Drugs.

137 U4 Anti-Corruption Resource Center, *supra* Part 2.

Article 2-2(c) which makes an offence transnational if its suspects, evidence, witnesses, proceeds, or equipment is situated in other States.

As mentioned above, the core principles for successful cooperation is 'direct contact and speedy response'. To ensure this principle, each party shall designate competent authorities such as the prosecution service as its central authority. At least one contact point within the central authority shall be available (Article 6-2, 8-1). Furthermore, parties shall adopt effective measures for a speedy exchange of basic information needed for early identification of suspects and offences (Article 7). The Model Treaty also allows for requests to be made via telecommunications, rather than in writing, in urgent circumstances (Article 10-2).

Extradition

For the purposes of this Model Treaty, extraditable offences are defined as those that are punishable under the laws of both parties by imprisonment or other deprivation of liberty for a period of one year or more, or by a more severe penalty (Article 12-1).

Although there is currently a clear trend toward elimination of the many grounds for refusal and limitations, this Model Treaty still intends to keep the traditional principles considering the disparity of legal systems in the Asia-Pacific. However, in order to enhance cooperation, we increased flexibility in some clauses. For example, if the requested party refuses to extradite its national, they shall submit the case without undue delay to its competent authorities for prosecution (Article 14-1).

Another point to note is that in the case where a party receives concurrent requests for extradition for the same person, the requested party may determine which party the person is to be extradited to at its discretion (Article 23).

Mutual Legal Assistance

The scope of assistance in the Model Treaty dictates that parties shall afford one another the widest measure of mutual legal assistance in investigations, prosecutions, and judicial proceedings in relation to any offence to which this Model Treaty applies (Article 25).

A few interesting points to note in the MLA clause of this Treaty are that a hearing may take place by video conferencing if a witness or expert is in a foreign country and unavailable to travel (Article 36). Also, competent authorities of a Party may exchange information relating to criminal matters without prior requests (Article 37-1). In this regard, in order to facilitate the rapid exchange of information, information available to the general public must be provided to the requesting party, while information not available to the general public under domestic law may be provided at the requested party's discretion (Article 37-2).

Transfer of Sentenced Persons

Both sentencing and administrating parties may request for the transfer of a sentenced person and the sentenced person may express his interest to either party upon being transferred under this Model

Treaty (Article 40).

Certain conditions have to be met in order for a transfer to take place. For example, the person must be a national of the administering party, the judgment must be final, and etc (Article 41). To guarantee sentenced persons' opportunities to freely express an interest in being transferred, the Model Treaty requires that the sentenced person be advised of the substance of this Model Treaty and that the voluntariness of the consent be verified (Article 42, 45).

Asset Recovery

While the extradition section deals with the recapturing of the offender and the MLA segment manages evidence, the asset recovery clause is made to strengthen existing cooperative systems relating to the proceeds of crime. In case of a request, the Model Treaty requires the requested party not only to confiscate the proceeds of crime, but also to take measures to identify, trace, freeze, or seize proceeds of crime, property, equipment, or other instrumentalities situated in their territory (Article 47).

Once a party confiscates the proceeds, they may dispose of it according to their laws. However, if so requested and to the extent permitted by domestic laws, the party may return the confiscated proceeds to the requesting party to compensate victims or to return such proceeds to the legitimate owners (Article 49).

Technical Assistance

The Model Treaty stresses the need for research and training programs to promote cooperation and to stimulate discussion on problems of mutual concern. The Model Treaty encourages the active reference and use of the programs such as the Prosecutors' Exchange Program and the Global Prosecutor's E-crime Network (GPEN), making efficient use of existing mechanisms (Article 50, 1-2).

The Model Treaty also stipulates the duty of all parties to assist developing countries in their fight against transnational crime (Article 51). There is special emphasis on the promotion of training and technical assistance in the field of digital forensics (Article 50-3) to prevent developing countries from being left behind.

Other Clauses of Interest

We should note that the Model Treaty shall not affect obligations under any other convention or treaty (Article 4-1). Therefore, it shall not be in conflict with any existing treaty or law. Instead, it should be applied as the legal basis for any kind of cooperation to which this Model Treaty applies in the absence of relevant conventions or treaties (Article 4-2).

Overall, the Model Treaty was formed with a less restrictive approach in mind because the countries in the Asia-pacific region differ in many aspects, including a wide disparity between each nation's legal system and infrastructure. Thus, any provision of this Model Treaty is subject to reservation so that each nation can apply it within their capacity (Article 53).

Working toward a United Nations Regional Convention

There is a clear need for an efficient and effective mechanism for cooperation in the field of criminal justice in the Asia-Pacific region. The IAP Model Treaty is the starting point preceding the eventual development of a convention between governments. In order to create an enforceable convention, each country would need to discuss at the governmental level and sign as parties to the treaty. However, this process takes too much time and endeavors. Before this lengthy and time-consuming process, the experts and main users of the convention should discuss and gather their opinions.

The Prosecution Service does not have the authority to bind its country in a treaty. The Model Treaty is not binding. It is just an ideal form of cooperation in criminal justice, which has been proposed, discussed and drafted among prosecutors in this region. Most prosecution services in the Asia and Pacific acknowledged, provided opinions, and agreed with the Model Treaty.

The Model Treaty is not an enforceable treaty now, but in the future, we hope that the governments of Asia-Pacific will gather together to further cultivate our efforts and develop the Model Treaty into a UN Regional Convention to meet the needs of the Asia-Pacific region more effectively and improve cooperation for criminal justice. By developing an Asia-Pacific Convention for Cooperation in Criminal

Justice, the Asia-Pacific region will be able to build a concrete foundation for efficient and effective cooperation based on the new initiatives of direct contact and speedy response.

Just as the Great Wall of China was not built in one day, the road toward a more unified mechanism in the Asia-Pacific will be long and challenging, requiring thoughtful discussions and extensive exchange of views among all parties concerned. A step-by-step approach will be critical in transforming Korea's proposal and work of IAP into a concrete cooperation framework that generates substantive outcomes in international criminal justice in the Asia-Pacific. In this way, we could have a global multilateral system for international cooperation in criminal justice in the future.

CONCLUSION

To cope with transnational crime, law enforcement agencies of each country agree that there is a need for new initiatives on international cooperation in criminal justice.

Universal jurisdiction on transnational crime could be the ultimate future goal of law enforcement agents in their fight against transnational crime. However, there is a long way to go. The concept of universal jurisdiction conflicts with the theory of sovereignty which must be respected in the international society. The Sovereignty of each country makes its own territorial jurisdiction for investigation and prosecution of crimes. Therefore, law enforcement agents are confined within their own territory regarding criminal activities. Meanwhile, criminals easily cross borderlines to commit criminal acts.

In this context, the best way to fight against transnational crimes is international cooperation between the law enforcement agencies of each country. For close and friendly cooperation, it is suggested to lower the barriers of sovereignty of each nation. We have to lower the fences of boundary and open a side door of friendship with neighbors. This is the new initiative on international cooperation in criminal justice. It is also a way to achieve 'direct contact and speedy response' between law enforcement agencies.

To obtain this goal, we need to establish new mechanisms and operation for international cooperation. A new framework of cooperation should be based on 'direct contact and speedy response.'

A multilateral treaty for the cooperation in criminal justice must be established in addition to the traditional bilateral approach of cooperation. Regional consolidation is also important for cooperation, especially in the Asia Pacific region. Therefore, we proposed the 'Asia-Pacific Convention for Cooperation in Criminal Justice.' It is now the IAP model treaty, but will be developed into a UN regional convention in the near future.

Under the umbrella of new mechanisms for cooperation, law enforcement agencies in each country can try to carry out the operations of international cooperation in their investigation and prosecution of transnational crimes. Under the new initiatives, the operation also must be based on 'direct contact and speedy response.' A network between law enforcement agents is essential for this work. The International Association of Prosecutors (IAP) and UN World Summit of Prosecutors General, Attorneys General, and Chief Prosecutors are recommended for prosecutors worldwide to network and cooperate. Through networking, they can build mutual trust for future cooperation.

It has always been my conviction that cooperation could be well operated only when based on Mutual Trust. Trust grows from Friendship, Friendship is brought up by Understanding, Understanding springs from Meeting.

We can pave the way to the new initiatives on international cooperation in criminal justice only through continuing efforts to make the new mechanism and operation for cooperation based on Direct Contact and Speedy Response.

APPENDIX

<Table A> Countries with which Korea has signed an Extradition Treaty

<Table B> Recent Extradition Statistics to and from Korea

<Table C> Countries with which Korea has signed a Mutual Legal Assistance Treaty

<Table D-1> Recent MLA Requests from Korea

<Table D-2> Recent MLA Requests to Korea

<Table E> Bilateral Treaties for Transfer of Sentenced Persons with Korea

<Chart F-1> Prisoner Transfer Requests from Korea

<Chart F-2> Prisoner Transfer Requests to Korea

<Section G> IAP Model Treaty: The Asia-Pacific Convention for Cooperation in Criminal Justice

<Section H-1> MOU between Korea and the United States

<Section H-2> MOU between Korea and Spain

<Chart I> Recent Statistics on MLA Requests in ASEAN Member Countries

<Table A>

Countries with which Korea has signed an Extradition Treaty

NO	Contracting Party	Date	Location	Entry into Force
1	Australia	1990.9.5	Seoul	1991.1.16
2	Philippines	1993.5.24	Seoul	1996.11.30
3	Spain	1994.1.17	Seoul	1995.2.15
4	Canada	1994.4.15	Ottawa	1995.1.29
5	Chile	1994.11.21	Seoul	1997.10.1
6	Argentina	1995.8.30	Buenos Aires	2000.11.9
7	Brazil	1995.9.1	Brasilia	2002.2.1
8	Paraguay	1996.7.9	Seoul	1996.12.29
9	Mexico	1996.11.29	Seoul	1997.12.27
10	U.S.A	1998.6.10	Washington D.C.	1999.12.20
11	Thailand	1999.4.26	Seoul	2001.2.15
12	Mongolia	1999.5.31	Ulan Bator	2000.1.27
13	China	2000.10.18	Seoul	2002.4.12
14	Indonesia	2000.11.28	Jakarta	2007.11.6
15	New Zealand	2001.5.15	Seoul	2002.4.17
16	Japan	2002.4.8	Seoul	2002.6.21
17	Uzbekistan	2003.2.12	Tashkent	2004.11.23
18	Vietnam	2003.9.15	Seoul	2005.4.19
19	Kazakhstan	2003.11.13	Seoul	2005.2.25*
20	Peru	2003.12.5	Lima	2005.11.16
21	Guatemala	2003.12.12	Guatemala City	2006.2.20
22	India	2004.10.5	New Delhi	2005.6.8
23	Costa Rica	2005.9.12	San Jose	2006.12.1*
24	France	2006.6.6	Paris	2008.6.1
25	Hong Kong	2006.6.26	Hong Kong	2007.2.11
26	Algeria	2007.2.17	Algiers	2008.10.24
27	South Africa	2007.5.3	Seoul	2008.2.29*
28	Kuwait	2007.6.14	Seoul	2008.2.29*
29	Bulgaria	2008.10.1	Sofia	2010.04.8
30	Cambodia	2009.10.22	Phnom Penh	Not in Force

* Yet to be ratified by the Contracting Party.

<Table B>

Recent Extradition Statistics to and from Korea

		91 ~99	00	01	02	03	04	05	06	07	08	09	10	Total
Extradition Requests from Korea to Abroad	US	1	6	1	6	1	4	6	14	9	8	8	12	78
	China		1		2	1	3	3	5	2	2	2	3	24
	Philippines	1					1	1	3	3	4	7	3	23
	Australia	6	1	1		2		1					1	12
	Canada	3								3		1	2	9
	Indonesia				1			1	1		1	3	1	8
	Japan						1		1	1	1	2		6
	Hong Kong (Macao)										1	4	1	6
	Peru		1				1			2		1		5
	Taiwan									5				5
	Germany	1				1				1			1	4
	Kazakhstan				1			1			1		1	4
	Argentina	3												3
	Spain	3												3
	Vietnam								1	1	1			3
	Chile	1					1							2
	New Zealand		1										1	2
	Thailand								2					2
	Kyrgyzstan										1	1		2
	Greece			1										1
	New Zealand				1									1
	Guatemala				1									1
	Denmark						1							1
	Uganda						1							1
	Russia							1						1
	Mongolia									1				1
	Mexico									1				1
	United Arab Emirates										1			1
	Colombia										1			1
	Cambodia										1			1
	Brazil	1				1					1	1	1	5
	Kenya												1	1
	Ecuador												1	1
	Total	20	10	3	11	7	12	14	27	29	24	31	28	218

		91 ~99	00	01	02	03	04	05	06	07	08	09	10	Total
Extradition Requests from Abroad to Korea	US		1	1	2	4		3			4	3	8	26
	Canada										1	1		
	China					3						1		4
	Japan				1		3	2	3	6	3	1	1	20
	Australia	1			1						3			5
	Germany	2	1								1			4
	Vietnam								1					1
	Hong Kong									1				1
	Argentina									1				1
	Thailand											1		1
	Uzbekistan												1	1
	Russia										1			1
	Sudan												1	1
	Total	3	1	1	1	2	4	2	1	7	6	4	10	68

<Table C>

Countries with which Korea has signed a Mutual Legal Assistance Treaty

NO	Contracting Party	Date	Location	Entry into Force
1	Australia	1992.8.25	Canberra	1993.12.19
2	U.S.A	1993.11.23	Washington D.C.	1997.5.23
3	Canada	1994.4.15	Ottawa	1995.2.1
4	France	1995.3.2	Paris	1997.3.8
5	China	1998.11.12	Beijing	2000.2.25
6	Hong Kong	1998.11.17	Hong Kong	2000.11.9
7	Russia	1995.5.28	Moscow	2001.8.10
8	Mongolia	1999.5.31	Ulan Bator	2000.1.27
9	New Zealand	1999.9.15	Wellington	2000.3.30
10	Indonesia	2002.3.30	Seoul	2003.6.30*
11	Brazil	2002.12.13	Brasilia	2006.2.8
12	Uzbekistan	2003.2.12	Tashkent	2004.11.23
13	Philippines	2003.6.3	Seoul	2008.11.17
14	Thailand	2003.8.25	Seoul	2005.4.6
15	Vietnam	2003.9.15	Seoul	2005.4.19
16	Kazakhstan	2003.11.13	Seoul	2005.2.25*
17	India	2004.10.5	New Delhi	2005.6.8
18	Mexico	2005.9.9	Mexico City	2007.1.18
19	Japan	2006.1.20	Tokyo	2007.1.26
20	Algeria	2006.3.12	Algiers	2007.6.15
21	Belgium	2007.1.17	Brussels	2008.2.29*
22	South Africa	2007.5.3	Seoul	2008.2.29*
23	Kuwait	2007.3.26	Kuwait City	2008.4.8
24	Peru	2007.9.9	Sydney	2008.9.29*
25	Bulgaria	2008.10.1	Sofia	2010.4.8
26	Spain	2009.3.23	Seoul	Not in Force
27	Argentina	2009.8.31	Seoul	2010.2.5*
28	Malaysia	2010.12.10	Putrajaya	Not in Force

* Yet to be ratified by the Contracting Party.

<Table D-1>

Recent MLA Requests from Korea

		03	04	05	06	07	08	09	10	Total
Requests from Korea	USA	10	3	7	8	12	21	22	16	99
	China	10	5	11	7	10	13	19	27	102
	Japan	2	2	4	4	12	8	11	8	51
	Hong Kong	3		4	3	2	2	4	3	21
	Canada		1	2			2	5	2	12
	Russia			1	6				4	11
	Philippines	1		1				3	1	6
	Bangladesh	1					1	2	3	7
	Switzerland	2					1			3
	UK	2				1				3
	Peru			2			1			3
	Taiwan		1				1	1		3
	Indonesia				1		1	1	2	5
	Cambodia						2	1	2	5
	Vietnam								3	3
	Argentina					1	1			2
	Kazakhstan						2			2
	Malaysia								3	3
	Thailand				1		1		3	5
	France				1		1			2
	Australia						2		4	6
	Greece			1						1
	Nigeria	1								1
	Netherlands						1			1
	New Zealand						1		2	3
	Denmark						1			1
	Lithuania		1							1
	Sri Lanka	1								1
	Spain						1			1
	United Arab Emirates						1		1	2
	Mongolia							1		1
	Turkey								1	1
	Germany								1	1
	Italy								1	1
	Total	33	13	33	31	38	65	70	87	370

<Table D-2>

Recent MLA Requests to Korea

		03	04	05	06	07	08	09	10	Total
Requests from Abroad	Japan	11	4	11	6	14	14	15	16	91
	Russia	12	3	9	8	7	6	4	8	57
	Argentina	4	2	4	2	6	2	2	3	25
	USA		1	4	3	3	4	4	4	23
	Poland	4	2	1		1	5	6	5	24
	India				5	4	1	1	4	15
	Switzerland	4	4					2	1	11
	Belgium	2	3	1	1	1	1	1	1	11
	Netherlands		1		4	3	1	1	3	13
	Uzbekistan	1	2	1	1	2	1	1	1	10
	Turkey	1			3	2		3	3	12
	Germany		1	1	3		2	1	1	9
	China			1		2	2	2	1	8
	Australia	2	1	1	2			1	3	10
	Brazil			1		1	4	1	2	9
	Sri Lanka				1	3	3			7
	South Africa	1	1	1			1	1		5
	Czech Republic		1		3			1		5
	Bulgaria				2		1	2	1	6
	Romania				1	1	2	1	2	7
	Mongolia			1		3			4	4
	France				3	1			1	5
	Ukraine	1		2						3
	Lithuania	1					1	1		3
	Portugal		1	1				1	1	4
	Mexico						3			3
	UK				1	1				2
	Philippines					2				2
	Kazakhstan			1		1			3	5
	Morocco			2						2
	Austria			1			1			2
	Mongolia				2					2
	Norway					1		1		2
	Italy					1	1			2
	Canada		1							1
	Kyrgyzstan	1							1	2
	Thailand	1								1
	Latvia	1								1
	Colombia			1						1
	New Zealand				1					1

		03	04	05	06	07	08	09	10	Total
Requests from Abroad	Israel				1					1
	Finland					1				1
	Spain						1		1	2
	Ecuador							1	1	2
	Hong Kong							1	1	2
	Vietnam							1		1
	Belarus							1	1	2
	Slovakia								2	2
	Saudi Arabia								1	1
	Peru								1	1
	Total	47	28	45	53	61	57	57	78	426

<Table E>

Bilateral Treaties for Transfer of Sentenced Persons with Korea

No.	Contracting Party	Date of Conclusion	Signatory	Date of Enforcement
1	Mongolia	2007. 5. 28	Minister of Foreign Affairs of both States	2008. 8. 23
2	China	2008. 5. 27	Minister of Foreign Affairs of both States	2009. 8. 5
3	Vietnam	2009. 5. 29	Vice-Minister of Foreign Affairs of both States	2010. 7. 30
4	Kuwait	2007. 6. 14	Minister of Justice of both States	Provisional Signing
5	India	2010. 1. 25	Korea's Minister of Foreign Affairs and India's Minister of Home Affairs	Provisional Signing

<Chart F-1>

Prisoner Transfer Requests from Korea

Overseas Transfer (Korea → Abroad)	2005	2006	2007	2008	2009	2010
Cases	-	-	US: 1 Japan: 1	UK: 1 Germany: 1 Netherlands: 1	US: 2	Mongolia: 1
Total	0	0	2	3	2	1

<Chart F-2>

Prisoner Transfer Requests to Korea

Domestic Transfer (Abroad → Korea)	2005	2006	2007	2008	2009	2010
Cases	-	-	Japan: 2 US: 1	Japan: 8	Japan: 6 US: 2	China: 1
Total	0	0	3	8	8	1

<Section G>

IAP Model Treaty: The Asia-Pacific Convention for Cooperation in Criminal Justice

Preamble

The Parties to this Treaty,

Concerned about the seriousness of problems and threats posed by transnational crime to the stability and security of all States in the Asia-Pacific region,

Convinced that regional cooperation is essential, especially among the competent authorities such as the prosecution service, and that a comprehensive and multilateral approach is required to prevent and combat transnational crime effectively,

Determined to strengthen regional cooperation in a more direct and speedy manner,

Bearing in mind that the prevention of and fight against transnational crime is a responsibility of all States and that they must cooperate with one another if their efforts in this area are to be effective,

Have agreed as follows:

Chapter 1. General Provision

Article 1. Statement of purpose

The purposes of this Treaty are:

(a) To stimulate and strengthen direct and speedy cooperation especially between the competent authorities of the Parties, such as the prosecution service, to prevent and combat transnational crime more efficiently and effectively;

(b) To facilitate the reintegration of sentenced persons into society by enabling them to serve their sentence in the country of which they are nationals; and

(c) To promote and support technical assistance that will facilitate international cooperation.

Article 2. Scope of application

1. This Treaty shall apply, except as otherwise stated herein, to extradition, mutual legal assistance, transfer of sentenced persons, asset recovery and technical assistance in the prevention of and fight against offences which are especially transnational in nature.
2. For the purpose of paragraph 1 of this article, an offence is considered transnational in nature if:
   (a) It is committed in more than one State;
   (b) It is committed in one State but a substantial part of its preparation, planning, direction or control takes place in

other States; or

(c) It is committed in one State but persons suspected of or sentenced for involvement in such offences, its evidences, witnesses, proceeds, equipment or instrumentalities are situated in other States.

Article 3. Relationship with other conventions or treaties

This Treaty shall not affect the obligations under any other convention or treaty, bilateral or multilateral.

Chapter 2. Promotion of Cooperation

Article 4. General principle

The Parties shall cooperate closely with one another, consistent with their respective domestic legal and administrative systems, to enhance the speed and effectiveness of cooperation between their competent authorities.

Article 5. Designation of central authority

1. Each Party shall designate a central authority that shall have the responsibility and power to receive and execute requests.
2. Each Party shall designate competent authorities such as the prosecution service as its central authority to ensure the speedy

and proper execution.

3. Requests covered by this Treaty and any communication related thereto shall be transmitted directly to the central authorities designated by the Parties.
4. The requirement of paragraph 3 of this article shall be without prejudice to the right of a Party to require that such requests and communications be addressed to it through diplomatic channels.

Article 6. Extra measures

Each Party shall, in particular, adopt effective measures:

1. To cooperate with other Parties in conducting inquiries with respect to offences covered by this Treaty concerning:
   (a) The identity, whereabouts and activities of persons suspected of involvement in such offences or the location of other persons concerned;
   (b) The movement of proceeds of crime or property derived from the commission of such offences; and
   (c) The movement of property, equipment or other instrumentalities used or intended for use in the commission of such offences.
2. To Facilitate the exchange of information among the Parties on patterns and trends in transnational crime and on successful practices for combating it.

Article 7. Contact point and liaison officers

1. Each Party shall put in place or appoint at least one contact point, within its office of central authority, which is available on a 24-hour/7-day basis to receive and process at all times requests referred to it.
2. The Parties shall adopt effective measures to facilitate active cooperation between their central authorities and to promote the exchange of personnel and other experts including the posting of liaison officers.

Article 8. Notification to others

1. The designation of the central authority and contact point shall be made at the time of ratification, acceptance or approval of this Treaty.
2. Each Party shall expeditiously notify the other Parties of any change in the designation of its central authority and contact point.

Article 9. Form of request

1. Requests shall be made in writing or, where possible, by any means capable of producing a written record, in a language acceptable to the requested Party, under conditions allowing that Party to establish authenticity.
2. In urgent circumstances and where agreed by the Parties,

requests may be made via telecommunications, but shall be confirmed in writing forthwith.

Chapter 3. Extradition

Article 10. General principle

1. The Parties agree to extradite to one another, upon request and subject to the provisions of this Treaty, any person who is wanted in the requesting Party for prosecution for an extraditable offence or for the imposition or enforcement of a sentence in respect of such an offence.
2. The Parties shall, subject to their domestic law, endeavor to expedite extradition procedures and to simplify evidentiary requirements relating thereto in respect of any offence to which this chapter applies.

Article 11. Extraditable offences

1. For the purposes of this Treaty, extraditable offences are offences that are punishable under the laws of both Parties by imprisonment or other deprivation of liberty for a period of one year or more, or by a more severe penalty.
2. In determining whether an offence is an offence against the law of both Parties:

   (a) It may not matter whether the laws of both Parties place the acts or omissions constituting the offence within the same category of offence or denominate the offence by the same terminology;

(b) The totality of the acts or omissions alleged against the person whose extradition is sought shall be taken into account and it may not matter whether, under the laws of both Parties, the constituent elements of the offence differ.

3. If extradition has been granted for an extraditable offence, it shall also be granted for any other offence specified in the request even if the latter offence is punishable by deprivation of liberty for a period of less than one year, provided that all other requirements for extradition are met.
4. Where the request for extradition relates to a person sentenced to deprivation of liberty by a court of the requesting Party for any extraditable offence, extradition may be denied if a period of less than four months remains to be served.

Article 12. Denial of extradition

1. Extradition may be denied in any of the following circumstances:
   (a) If the offence for which extradition is requested is regarded by the requested Party as an offence of a political nature;
   (b) If the requested Party has substantial grounds for believing that the request for extradition has been made for the purpose of prosecuting or punishing a person on account of that person's race, sex, religion, nationality, ethnic origin or political opinions or that that person's position may be

prejudiced for any of those reasons;

(c) If the person whose extradition is requested had been convicted or acquitted in the requested Party for the offence for which extradition is requested; or

(d) If the person whose extradition is requested has, under the law of either Party, become immune from prosecution or punishment for any reason, including lapse of time or amnesty.

2. The Parties may not refuse a request for extradition on the sole ground that the offence is considered to involve fiscal matters.

3. Before refusing extradition, the requested Party shall, where appropriate, consult with the requesting Party to provide it with ample opportunity to present its opinions and to provide information relevant to its allegation.

Article 13. Extradition of nationals

1. A Party in whose territory an alleged offender is found, if it does not extradite such person in respect of an offence to which this chapter applies solely on the ground that he or she is one of its nationals, shall, at the request of the Party seeking extradition, be obliged to submit the case without undue delay to its competent authorities for the purpose of prosecution. Those authorities shall take their decision and conduct their proceedings in the same manner as under the domestic law of that Party. The Parties concerned shall cooperate with each other, in particular on procedural and evidentiary aspects, to

ensure the efficiency of such prosecution.

2. Whenever a Party is permitted under its domestic law to extradite or otherwise surrender one of its nationals only upon the condition that the person will be returned to that Party to serve the sentence imposed as a result of the trial or proceedings for which the extradition or surrender of the person was sought and that Party and the Party seeking the extradition of the person agree with this option and other terms that they may deem appropriate, such conditional extradition or surrender shall be sufficient to discharge the obligation set forth in paragraph 1 of this article.
3. If extradition, sought for purposes of enforcing a sentence, is refused because the person sought is a national of the requested Party, the requested Party may, if its domestic law so permits and in conformity with the requirements of such law, upon application of the requesting Party, consider the enforcement of the sentence that has been imposed under the domestic law of the requesting Party or the remainder thereof.

Article 14. Required documents

1. A request for extradition shall be accompanied by the following:
   (a) In all cases,
      (i) As accurate a description as possible of the person sought, together with any other information that may help to establish that person's identity, nationality and location; and

(ii) The text of the relevant provision of the law creating the offence or, where necessary, a statement of the law relevant to the offence and a statement of the penalty that can be imposed for the offence;

(b) If the person is accused of an offence, by a warrant issued by a court or other competent judicial authority for the arrest of the person or a certified copy of that warrant, a statement of the offence for which extradition is requested and a description of the acts or omissions constituting the alleged offence, including an indication of the time and place of its commission;

(c) If the person has been convicted of an offence, by a statement of the offence for which extradition is requested and a description of the acts or omissions constituting the offence and by the original or certified copy of the judgment or any other document setting out the conviction and the sentence imposed, the fact that the sentence is enforceable, and the extent to which the sentence remains to be served;

(d) If the person has been convicted of an offence in his or her absence, in addition to the documents set out in paragraph 1(c) of this article, by a statement as to the legal means available to the person to prepare his or her defense or to have the case retried in his or her presence;

(e) If the person has been convicted of an offence but no sentence has been imposed, by a statement of the offence for which extradition is requested and a description of the acts or omissions constituting the offence and by a document setting out the conviction and a statement affirming that there is an intention to impose a sentence.

2. The documents submitted in support of a request for extradition shall be accompanied by a translation into the language of the requested Party or in another language acceptable to that Party.

Article 15. Provisional arrest

Subject to the provisions of its domestic law and its extradition treaties, the requested Party may, upon being satisfied that the circumstances so warrant and are urgent and at the request of the requesting Party, take a person whose extradition is sought and who is present in its territory into custody or take other appropriate measures to ensure his or her presence at extradition proceedings.

Article 16. Guarantee of procedural rights

Any person regarding whom extradition proceedings are being carried out in connection with any of the offences to which this chapter applies shall be guaranteed fair treatment at all stages of the proceedings, including enjoyment of all the rights and guarantees provided by the domestic law of the Party in the territory of which that person is present.

Article 17. Decision on the request

1. The requested Party shall deal with the request for extradition pursuant to procedures provided by its own law, and shall promptly communicate its decision to the requesting Party.
2. Reasons shall be given for any complete or partial refusal of the request.

Article 18. Surrender of the person

1. Upon being informed that extradition has been granted, the Parties shall, without undue delay, arrange for the surrender of the person sought and the requested Party shall inform the requesting Party of the length of time for which the person sought was detained with a view to surrender.
2. The person shall be removed from the territory of the requested Party within such reasonable period as the requested Party specifies and, if the person is not removed within that period, the requested Party may release the person and may refuse to extradite that person for the same offence.
3. If circumstances beyond its control prevent a Party from surrendering or removing the person to be extradited, it shall notify the other Party. The two Parties shall mutually decide upon a new date of surrender, and the provisions of paragraph 2 of this article shall apply.

Article 19. Postponed or conditional surrender

1. The requested Party may, after making its decision on the request for extradition, postpone the surrender of a person sought, in order to proceed against that person, or, if that person has already been convicted, in order to enforce a sentence imposed for an offence other than that for which extradition is sought. In such a case the requested Party shall advise the requesting Party accordingly.
2. The requested Party may instead of postponing surrender, temporarily surrender the person sought to the requesting Party in accordance with conditions to be determined between the Parties.

Article 20. Surrender of property

1. To the extent permitted under the law of the requested Party and subject to the rights of third Parties, which shall be duly respected, all property found in the requested Party that has been acquired as a result of the offence or that may be required as evidence shall, if the requesting Party so requests, be surrendered if extradition is granted.
2. The said property may, if the requesting Party so requests, be surrendered to the requesting Party even if the extradition agreed to cannot be carried out.
3. When the said property is liable to seizure or confiscation in the requested Party, it may retain it or temporarily hand it over.

4. Where the law of the requested Party or the protection of the rights of third parties so requires, any property so surrendered shall be returned to the requested Party free of charge after the completion of the proceedings, if that Party so requests.

Article 21. Rule of specialty

1. A person extradited under this Treaty shall not be proceeded against, sentenced, detained, re-extradited to a third Party, or subjected to any other restriction of personal liberty in the territory of the requesting Party for any offence committed before surrender other than:
   (a) An offence for which extradition was granted; and
   (b) Any other offence in respect of which the requested Party consents. Consent shall be given if the offence for which it is requested is itself subject to extradition in accordance with this Treaty.
2. A request for the consent of the requested Party under this Treaty shall be accompanied by the documents mentioned in paragraph 1 of article 15 and a legal record of any statement made by the extradited person with respect to the offence.
3. Paragraph 1 of this article shall not apply if the person has had an opportunity to leave the requesting Party and has not done so within 30 days of final discharge in respect of the offence for which that person was extradited or if the person has voluntarily returned to the territory of the requesting Party after leaving it.

Article 22. Concurrent requests

If a Party receives requests for extradition for the same person from more than one Party, it shall, at its discretion, determine to which of those Parties the person is to be extradited.

Article 23. Costs

1. The requested Party shall meet the cost of any proceedings in its jurisdiction arising out of a request for extradition.
2. The requested Party shall also bear the costs incurred in its territory in connection with the seizure and handing over of property, or the arrest and detention of the person whose extradition is sought.
3. The requesting Party shall bear the costs incurred in conveying the person from the territory of the requested Party, including transit costs.

Chapter 4. Mutual Legal Assistance

Article 24. General principle

The Parties shall afford one another the widest measure of mutual legal assistance in investigations, prosecutions and judicial proceedings in relation to any offence to which this Treaty applies.

Article 25. Scope of assistance

Mutual legal assistance to be afforded in accordance with this chapter may be requested for any of the following purposes:

(a) Taking evidence or statements from persons;

(b) Effecting service of judicial documents;

(c) Executing searches and seizures, and freezing;

(d) Examining objects and sites;

(e) Providing information, evidentiary items and expert evaluations;

(f) Providing originals or certified copies of relevant documents and records, including government, bank, financial, corporate or business records;

(g) Identifying or tracing proceeds of crime, property, instrumentalities or other things for evidentiary purposes;

(h) Facilitating the voluntary appearance of persons in the requesting Party;

(i) The recovery of assets; or

(j) Any other type of assistance that is not contrary to the domestic law of the requested Party.

Article 26. Refusal of assistance

1. Mutual legal assistance may be refused if:

(a) The request is not made in conformity with the provisions of this chapter;

(b) The requested Party considers that execution of the request is likely to prejudice its sovereignty, security, ordre public or other essential interests;

(c) The offence is regarded by the requested Party as being of a political nature;

(d) There are substantial grounds for believing that the request for assistance has been made for the purpose of prosecuting or punishing a person on account of that person's race, sex, religion, nationality, ethnic origin or political opinions or that that person's position may be prejudiced for any of those reasons;

(e) If the authorities of the requested Party would be prohibited by its domestic law from carrying out the action requested with regard to any similar offence, had it been subject to investigation, prosecution or judicial proceedings under their own jurisdiction; or

(f) If it would be contrary to the legal system of the requested Party relating to mutual legal assistance for the request to be granted.

2. The Parties may not decline to render mutual legal assistance pursuant to this chapter on the ground of bank secrecy.
3. The Parties may not refuse a request for mutual legal assistance on the sole ground that the offence is considered to involve fiscal matters.
4. Reasons shall be given for any refusal of mutual legal assistance.

Article 27. Dual criminality

The Parties may decline to render mutual legal assistance pursuant to this chapter on the ground of absence of dual criminality. However, the requested Party may, when it deems appropriate, provide assistance, to the extent it decides at its discretion, irrespective of whether the conduct would constitute an offence under the domestic law of the requested Party.

Article 28. Contents of requests

1. A request for mutual legal assistance shall contain:
   (a) The identity of the authority making the request;
   (b) The subject matter and nature of the investigation, prosecution or judicial proceeding to which the request relates and the name and functions of the authority conducting the investigation, prosecution or judicial proceeding;
   (c) A summary of the relevant facts, except in relation to requests for the purpose of service of judicial documents;
   (d) A description of the assistance sought and details of any particular procedure that the requesting Party wishes to be followed;
   (e) Where possible, the identity, location and nationality of any person concerned; and
   (f) The purpose for which the evidence, information or action is sought.

2. The requested Party may request additional information when it appears necessary for the execution of the request in accordance with its domestic law or when it can facilitate such execution.

Article 29. Execution of requests

1. A request shall be executed in accordance with the domestic law of the requested Party and, to the extent not contrary to the domestic law of the requested Party and where possible, in accordance with the procedures specified in the request.
2. The requested Party shall execute the request for mutual legal assistance as soon as possible and shall take as full account as possible of any deadlines suggested by the requesting Party and for which reasons are given, preferably in the request. The requesting Party may make reasonable requests for information on the status and progress of measures taken by the requested Party to satisfy its request. The requested Party shall respond to reasonable requests by the requesting Party on progress of its handling of the request. The requesting Party shall promptly inform the requested Party when the assistance sought is no longer required.

Article 30. Postponement of assistance

Mutual legal assistance may be postponed by the requested Party on the ground that it interferes with an ongoing investigation, prosecution or judicial proceeding.

Article 31. Consultation prior to refusal or postponement

Before refusing a request or postponing its execution, the requested Party shall consult with the requesting Party to consider whether assistance may be granted subject to such terms and conditions as it deems necessary. If the requesting Party accepts assistance subject to those conditions, it shall comply with the conditions.

Article 32. Limitation on use of evidence obtained

The requesting Party shall not transmit or use information or evidence furnished by the requested Party for investigations, prosecutions or judicial proceedings other than those stated in the request without the prior consent of the requested Party. Nothing in this article shall prevent the requesting Party from disclosing in its proceedings information or evidence that is exculpatory to an accused person. In the latter case, the requesting Party shall notify the requested Party prior to the disclosure and, if so requested, consult with the requested Party. If, in an exceptional case, advance notice is not possible, the requesting Party shall inform the requested Party of the disclosure without delay.

Article 33. Protection of confidentiality

The requesting Party may require that the requested Party keep confidential the fact and substance of the request, except to the extent necessary to execute the request. If the requested Party cannot comply with the requirement of confidentiality, it shall promptly inform the requesting Party.

Article 34. Transfer of persons in custody

A person who is being detained or is serving a sentence in the territory of a Party whose presence in another Party is requested for purposes of identification, testimony or otherwise providing assistance in obtaining evidence for investigations, prosecutions or judicial proceedings in relation to offences covered by this Treaty may be transferred if the following conditions are met:

(a) The person freely gives his or her informed consent; and

(b) The competent authorities of both Parties agree, subject to such conditions as those Parties may deem appropriate.

Article 35. Video conference

Wherever possible and consistent with fundamental principles of domestic law, when an individual is in the territory of a Party and has to be heard as a witness or expert by the judicial authorities of another Party, the first Party may, at the request of the other, permit the hearing to take place by video conference if it is not possible or desirable for the individual in question to appear in person in the territory of the requesting Party. The Parties may agree that the hearing shall be conducted by a judicial authority of the requesting Party and attended by a judicial authority of the requested Party.

Article 36. Exchange of information

1. Without prejudice to domestic law, the competent authorities of a Party may, without prior request, transmit information relating to criminal matters to a competent authority in another Party where they believe that such information could assist the authority in undertaking or successfully concluding inquiries and criminal proceedings or could result in a request formulated by the latter Party pursuant to this Treaty.
2. In order to facilitate the secure and rapid exchange of information, the requested Party:
   (a) Shall provide to the requesting Party copies of government records, documents or information in its possession that under its domestic law are available to the general public;
   (b) May, at its discretion, provide to the requesting Party in whole, in part or subject to such conditions as it deems appropriate, copies of any government records, documents or information in its possession that under its domestic law are not available to the general public.

Article 37. Costs

The ordinary costs of executing a request shall be borne by the requested Party, unless otherwise determined by the Parties. If expenses of a substantial or extraordinary nature are or will be required to execute the request, the Parties shall consult in advance to determine the terms and conditions under which the request shall be executed as well as the manner in which the costs shall be borne.

Chapter 5. Transfer of Sentenced Persons

Article 38. Definitions

For the purposes of this chapter:

(a) "Sentence" means any punishment or measure involving deprivation of liberty ordered by a court for a limited or unlimited period of time on account of a criminal offence;

(b) "Judgment" means a decision or order of a court imposing a sentence;

(c) "Sentencing Party" means the Party in which the sentence was imposed on the person who may be, or has been, transferred;

(d) "Administering Party" means the Party to which the sentenced person may be, or has been, transferred in order to serve his or her sentence.

Article 39. General principle

1. The Parties undertake to afford each other the widest measure of cooperation in respect of the transfer of sentenced persons in accordance with the provisions of this Treaty.
2. A person sentenced in the territory of a Party may be transferred to the territory of another Party, in accordance with the provisions of this Treaty, in order to serve the sentence imposed

on him or her. To that end, he or she may express his interest to the sentencing Party or to the administering Party in being transferred under this Treaty.

3. Transfer may be requested by either the sentencing Party or the administering Party.

Article 40. Conditions for transfer

1. A sentenced person may be transferred under this Treaty only on the following conditions:
   (a) If that person is a national of the administering Party;
   (b) If the judgment is final;
   (c) If, at the time of receipt of the request for transfer, the sentenced person still has at least six months of the sentence to serve or if the sentence is indeterminate;
   (d) If the transfer is consented to by the sentenced person or, where in view of his or her age or physical or mental condition one of the two Parties considers it necessary, by the sentenced person's legal representative;
   (e) If the acts or omissions on account of which the sentence has been imposed constitute a criminal offence according to the law of the administering Party or would constitute a criminal offence if committed on its territory; and
   (f) If the sentencing and administering Parties agree to the transfer.
2. In exceptional cases, the Parties may agree to a transfer even if the time to be served by the sentenced person is less than that

specified in paragraph 1(c) of this article.

Article 41. Obligation to furnish information

1. Any sentenced person to whom this Treaty may apply shall be informed by the sentencing Party of the substance of this Treaty.
2. If the sentenced person has expressed an interest to the sentencing Party in being transferred under this Treaty, that Party shall so inform the administering Party as soon as practicable after the judgment becomes final.
3. The information shall include:
   (a) The name, date and place of birth of the sentenced person;
   (b) His or her address, if any, in the administering Party;
   (c) A statement of the facts upon which the sentence was based; and
   (d) The nature, duration and date of commencement of the sentence.
4. If the sentenced person has expressed his or her interest to the administering Party, the sentencing Party shall, on request, communicate to the Party the information referred to in paragraph 3 above.
5. The sentenced person shall be informed, in writing, of any action taken by the sentencing Party or by the administering Party under the preceding paragraphs, as well as of any decision taken by either Party on a request for transfer.

Article 42. Prompt replies

The requested Party shall promptly inform the requesting Party of its decision whether or not to agree to the requested transfer.

Article 43. Supporting documents

1. The administering Party, if requested by the sentencing Party, shall furnish it with:
   (a) A document or statement indicating that the sentenced person is a national of that Party; and
   (b) A copy of the relevant law of the administering Party which provides that the acts or omissions on account of which the sentence has been imposed in the sentencing Party constitute a criminal offence according to the law of the administering Party, or would constitute a criminal offence if committed on its territory;
2. If a transfer is requested, the sentencing Party shall provide the following documents to the administering Party, unless either Party has already indicated that it will not agree to the transfer:
   (a) A certified copy of the judgment and the law on which it is based;
   (b) A statement indicating how much of the sentence has already been served, including information on any pre-trial detention, remission, and any other factor relevant to the enforcement of the sentence;
   (c) A declaration containing the consent to the transfer as

referred to in paragraph 1(d) of article 41; and

(d) Whenever appropriate, any medical or social reports on the sentenced person, information about his and her treatment in the sentencing Party, and any recommendation for his or her further treatment in the administering Party.

3. Either Party may ask to be provided with any of the documents or statements referred to in paragraphs 1 or 2 above before making a request for transfer or taking a decision on whether or not to agree to the transfer.

Article 44. Consent and its verification

1. The sentencing Party shall ensure that the person required to give consent to the transfer in accordance with paragraph 1(d) of article 41 does so voluntarily and with full knowledge of the legal consequences thereof. The procedure for giving such consent shall be governed by the law of the sentencing Party.
2. The sentencing Party shall afford an opportunity to the administering Party to verify through a consul or other official agreed upon with the administering Party, that the consent is given in accordance with the conditions set out in paragraph 1 above.

Article 45. Costs

Any costs incurred in the application of this Treaty shall be borne by the administering Party, except costs incurred exclusively in the territory of the sentencing Party.

Chapter 6. Asset Recovery

Article 46. General principle

1. A Party that has received a request from another Party having jurisdiction over an offence covered by this Treaty for confiscation of proceeds of crime, property, equipment or other instrumentalities situated in its territory may, to the greatest extent possible within its domestic legal system:
   (a) Submit the request to its competent authorities for the purpose of obtaining an order of confiscation and, if such an order is granted, give effect to it; or
   (b) Submit to its competent authorities, with a view to giving effect to it to the extent requested, an order of confiscation issued by a court in the territory of the requesting Party insofar as it relates to proceeds of crime, property, equipment or other instrumentalities situated in the territory of the requested Party.
2. Following a request made by another Party having jurisdiction over an offence covered by this Treaty, the requested Party may take measures to identify, trace and freeze or seize proceeds of crime, property, equipment or other instrumentalities for the purpose of eventual confiscation to be ordered either by the requesting Party or, pursuant to a request under paragraph 1 of

this article, by the requested Party.

Article 47. Contents of requests

The provisions of Chapter 4 of this Treaty are applicable, mutatis mutandis, to this article. In addition to the information specified in paragraph 1 of article 29, requests made pursuant to this article shall contain:

(a) In the case of a request pertaining to paragraph 1(a) of article 47, a description of the property to be confiscated and a statement of the facts relied upon by the requesting Party sufficient to enable the requested State Party to seek the order under its domestic law;

(b) In the case of a request pertaining to paragraph 1(b) of article 47, a legally admissible copy of an order of confiscation upon which the request is based issued by the requesting Party, a statement of the facts and information as to the extent to which execution of the order is requested;

(c) In the case of a request pertaining to paragraph 2 of article 47, a statement of the facts relied upon by the requesting Party and a description of the actions requested.

Article 48. Disposal of confiscated proceeds of crime

1. Proceeds of crime confiscated by a Party pursuant to paragraph 1 of article 47 shall be disposed of by that Party in accordance with its domestic law and administrative procedures.

2. When acting on the request made by another Party in accordance with article 47, the Parties may, to the extent permitted by domestic law and if so requested, give priority consideration to returning the confiscated proceeds of crime to the requesting Party so that it can give compensation to the victims of the crime or return such proceeds of crime to their legitimate owners.
3. The provisions of this chapter shall not be construed to prejudice the rights of bona fide third parties.

Chapter 7. Technical Assistance

Article 49. Training and technical assistance

1. Each Party shall, to the extent necessary, initiate, develop or improve specific research and training programmes for its law enforcement personnel, including prosecutors and other personnel charged with the prevention, detection and control of the offences covered by this Treaty.
2. The Parties shall assist one another in planning and implementing research and training programmes designed to share expertise in the areas referred to in paragraph 1 of this article and to that end shall also, when appropriate, use regional and international programmes, conferences and seminars, such as the Prosecutor's Exchange Program("PEP") and Global Prosecutors E-crime Network("GPEN") of the International

Association of Prosecutors, to promote cooperation and to stimulate discussion on problems of mutual concern.

3. The Parties shall promote training and technical assistance that will facilitate international cooperation, especially in the field of digital forensics. Such training and technical assistance may include language training, secondments and exchanges between personnel in central and competent authorities or agencies with relevant responsibilities.

Article 50. Economic development and technical assistance

1. The Parties shall make concrete efforts to the extent possible and in coordination with each other, as well as with international and regional organizations:
   (a) To enhance their cooperation at various levels with developing countries, with a view to strengthening the capacity of the latter to prevent and combat transnational crime;
   (b) To enhance financial and material assistance to support the efforts of developing countries to fight transnational crime effectively and to help them implement this Treaty successfully;
   (c) To provide technical and financial assistance to developing countries and countries with economies in transition to assist them in meeting their needs for the implementation of necessary legislation, technology and facilities of digital forensic investigation;

(d) To encourage and persuade one another and financial institutions as appropriate to join them in efforts in accordance with this article, in particular by providing more training programmes and modern equipment to developing countries in order to assist them in achieving the objectives of this Treaty.

2. To the extent possible, these measures shall be without prejudice to existing foreign assistance commitments or to other financial cooperation arrangements at the bilateral, regional or international level.

Chapter 8. Final Provisions

Article 51. Entry into force and termination

1. This Treaty is subject to ratification, acceptance, approval or accession. The instruments of ratification, acceptance, approval or accession shall be deposited with a Party which is designated as the Depository State.
2. This Treaty shall enter into force for each Party ratifying, accepting, approving or acceding to it on the date of the deposit of its instrument of ratification, acceptance, approval or accession.
3. This Treaty shall apply to requests made after its entry into force, even if the relevant acts or omissions occurred prior to that date.

4. Any Party may denounce this Treaty by written notification to the Depository State. Denunciation shall take effect six months following the date on which notification is received by the Depository State.

IN WITNESS WHEREOF, the undersigned plenipotentiaries, being duly authorized thereto by their respective Governments, have signed this Treaty.

<Section H-1>

MOU between Korea and the United States

MEMORANDUM OF UNDERSTANDING
ON MUTUAL COOPERATION
BETWEEN THE SUPREME PROSECUTION SERVICE
OF THE REPUBLIC OF KOREA
AND
THE DEPARTMENT OF HOMELAND SECURITY
IMMIGRATION AND CUSTOMS ENFORCEMENT
OF THE UNITED STATES OF AMERICA

The Supreme Prosecution Service of the Republic of Korea and the Department of Homeland Security Immigration and Customs Enforcement of the United States of America(together, "the Participants") have the responsibility, among other things, to investigate individuals involved in money laundering, violating intellectual property rights, proliferation, cyber crimes, and human smuggling and trafficking.

The Participants recognize that bi-national cooperation may facilitate the investigation of these crimes in the Republic of Korea and the United States.

The Participants seek to develop a comprehensive investigative response to the violation of particular criminal laws in their respective countries which should involve the sharing of information and the development of protocols for such exchanges.

This approach is not intended to affect in any way the obligations and practices currently in place or that may otherwise be established in consultations under the Mutual Legal Assistance Treaty between the Republic of Korea and the United States.

In particular, the Participants endeavor to cooperate in the following areas:

1. Anti-Money Laundering Cooperation. The Participants intend to increase information sharing to combat money laundering offenses, including bulk cash smuggling, and to cooperate in identifying, seizing, confiscating, and forfeiting criminal proceeds, as appropriate.

2. Intellectual Property Rights Protection Cooperation. The Participants believe cooperation in fighting against the violation of intellectual property rights is to the benefit of both Republic of Korea and United States law enforcement agencies.

3. Counter Proliferation Investigations. The Participants intend to cooperate in the sharing of best practices and law enforcement techniques in counter proliferation investigations.

4. Cyber Crimes Investigation. Both Participants intend to cooperate in the sharing of best practices and law enforcement techniques in the investigation of cyber and computer related crimes.

5. Anti-human Trafficking and Smuggling Investigations. The Participants are to endeavor to cooperate in the sharing of best practices and law enforcement techniques in the investigation of human smuggling and trafficking investigations.

Signed at Seoul, Korea on September 13, 2010 in duplicate, in the Korean and English languages.

FOR THE SUPREME PROSECUTION SERVICE OF THE REPUBLIC OF KOREA	**FOR U.S. DEPARTMENT OF HOMELAND SECURITY**
Joon Gyu Kim	**John Morton**
Prosecutor General	Assistant Secretary for Homeland Security Director, U.S. Immigration and Customs Enforcement

<Section H-2>

MOU between Korea and Spain

MEMORANDUM OF UNDERSTANDING ON COOPERATION

BETWEEN

THE SUPREME PROSECUTORS' OFFICE OF THE REPUBLIC OF KOREA

AND

THE SPANISH GENERAL PROSECUTOR'S OFFICE OF THE KINGDOM OF SPAIN

IN COMBATING TRANSNATIONAL CRIME AND LAUNDERING OF THE PROCEEDS FROM CRIME

The Supreme Prosecutors' Office of the Republic of Korea and the Spanish General Prosecutor's Office of the Kingdom of Spain, hereinafter referred to as the "Signatory Institutions",

- aiming at strengthening and developing mutual relations in regard to international cooperation and fighting crime and laundering of the proceeds of crime as provided under this Memorandum of Understanding and pursuant to their respective authorities, in compliance at all times with both States' legislation and international commitments;

- being governed by principles of equality, mutual understanding and mutual interests, fulfilment of obligations in good faith and respect for human rights;

HAVE REACHED THE FOLLOWING UNDERSTANDING:

1. The Signatory Institutions, within the framework of their competence and in compliance with legislation of their respective States, will cooperate in combating transnational crime and laundering of the proceeds from crime.

2. Cooperation within the framework of this Memorandum will be carried out by the Signatory Institutions through the exchange of information and documents concerning crimes with international relations and persons involved in them.

The Signatory Institutions, following the requirements of confidentiality, will exchange if possible, information on nationals of their states who are on trial for committed crimes related to transnational crimes and also the laundering of the proceeds of crime.

3. The Signatory Institutions will take every possible measure, within the limits of their powers, in order to assist in the effective and timely fulfilment of any request on legal assistance in criminal matters related to transnational crimes and laundering of the proceeds, if such requests have been accepted by competent authorities of the requested State.

4. The Signatory Institutions will develop professional contacts and relations between their members in order to effectively update their experiences and to exchange information and data on their current legislation, and in particular to exchange the texts of legislative and other regulatory enactments, including analytical materials, statistical data, and reports on combating transnational crime and laundering of the proceeds from crimes.

5. For the purpose of implementation of this Memorandum, the Signatory Institutions will contact each other directly, with full respect to the channels provided for in bilateral treaties or Conventions signed by both States.

For the direct contact, the Signatory Institutions will use the following addresses and communications means:

Korean Signatory Institution:

Supreme Prosecutors' Office of the Republic of Korea
706, Banpo-ro, Seocho-gu, Seoul, Korea
Fax: +82 2 535 0807
e-mail: koreapros@spo.go.kr

Spanish Signatory Institution:

Unidad de Cooperación Internacional de la Fiscalía General del Estado.
C/ Ortega y Gasset, 57
28071-Madrid.
Tel: +34 91 423 08 20
Fax: +34 91 423 08 21
e-mail: internacional.fge@fiscal.es

6. Cooperation within the framework of this Memorandum will be carried out on the basis of requests for information. Each Signatory Institution may forward to the other Signatory Institution information without prior request when it considers that such information might assist the receiving Signatory Institution in initiating or carrying out investigations.

7. The requests for information and the relevant answers will be sent directly, in the written form, and in the language of the requesting Signatory Institution with a translation in the language of the requested Signatory Institution, or a translation in English. Such requests may be sent by e-mail, facsimile communications channels, or other technical communications.

8. The requests for information will be fulfilled by each Signatory Institution in compliance with legislation of its own Country. In case it is impossible to fulfil a request, the requested Signatory Institution will immediately inform the requesting Signatory Institution of the reasons which prevent such fulfilment.

9. The Signatory Institution which provides information and documents in accordance with the provisions of this Memorandum may request the other Signatory Institution to ensure that they be kept confidential when used.

If the requesting Signatory Institution needs to use such information and materials for trial purposes, it will submit the request for legal assistance in compliance with the rules established by international law and its internal legislation.

10. All issues related to interpretation and implementation of this Memorandum will be decided by the Signatory Institutions according to the principles of mutual understanding and respect. At any time this Memorandum may be amended and changed by common agreement of the Signatory Institutions.

11. This Memorandum does not create any new interstate legal obligations for the Signatory Institutions and their States and does not affect any of their present international obligations. Cooperation within the framework of this Memorandum will be carried out through the constant will of the Signatory Institutions for reaching practical decisions in the field of combating transnational crime and in the partnership spirit which characterizes this document.

12. This Memorandum will come into effect on the date of signature. This Memorandum is concluded for an unlimited period of time. Either Signatory Institution may denounce this Memorandum by giving written notice to the other Signatory Institution. In such case, the Memorandum will terminate six months from the date of receipt of the denunciation notice by the other Signatory Institution.

Signed in Seoul, Republic of Korea, on June 28, 2011 in two originals in each language Korean, Spanish, and English, all texts being equally valid. In case of divergences in interpretation, the English text will prevail.

FOR THE SUPREME PROSECUTORS' OFFICE OF THE REPUBLIC OF KOREA	FOR THE SPANISH GENERAL PROSECUTOR'S OFFICE OF THE KINGDOM OF SPAIN
Joon Gyu Kim	**Cándido Conde-Pumpido Tourón**
PROSECUTOR GENERAL REPUBLIC OF KOREA	PROSECUTOR GENERAL KINGDOM OF SPAIN

<Chart I>

Recent Statistics on MLA Requests in ASEAN Member Countries

STATISTICS DATABASE

TREATY ON MUTUAL LEGAL ASSISTANCE IN CRIMINAL MATTERS

(LAST UPDATED: 18 November 2010)

Note :

The information listed below is as provided by the respective Treaty Parties.

(a) Requests received by Treaty Party under the Treaty

State	Year						Total
	2005	2006	2007	2008	2009	2010	
Brunei	-	-	-	-	1	4	5
Cambodia	-	-	-	-	-	-	0
Indonesia	-	-	-	-	1	1	2
Lao PDR	-	-	-	-	-	-	0
Malaysia	0	0	1	2	1	-	4
Myanmar	-	-	-	-	-	-	0
Philippines	-	-	-	-	-	-	0
Singapore*	1	8	7	15	8	8	47
Thailand**	-	-	-	-	-	5	5
Vietnam	-	-	-	-	-	3	3

*These statistics include requests from other ASEAN countries which have been made outside the framework of the Treaty on Mutual Legal Assistance in Criminal Matters.

**Thailand has not ratified the Treaty yet.

(b) Requests made by Treaty Party under the Treaty

State	Year						Total
	2005	2006	2007	2008	2009	2010	
Brunei	-	-	-	-	-	1	1
Cambodia	-	-	-	-	-	-	0
Indonesia	-	-	-	-	2	-	2
Lao PDR	-	-	-	-	-	-	0
Malaysia	0	1	3	5	6	3	18
Myanmar	-	-	-	-	-	-	0
Philippines	-	-	-	-	-	-	0
Singapore*	0	0	1	0	1		2
Thailand**	-	-	-	-	-	-	0
Vietnam	-	-	-	-	-	13	13

*These statistics include requests to other ASEAN countries which may have been made outside the framework of the Treaty on Mutual Legal Assistance in Criminal Matters.

**Thailand has not ratified the Treaty yet.

ABOUT THE AUTHORS

Joon Gyu Kim

Joon Gyu Kim is an attorney practicing in Seoul, Korea. Mr. Kim serves clients in association with domestic and international law firms and lawyers. His primary focus is in the area of overseas dispute resolution of corporations.

Before establishing his own law firm, Kim & associations, Mr. Kim served as a prosecutor for thirty years. As a prosecutor, he handled numerous cases and special investigations on economic crimes and corruption. Mr. Kim served as a Chief Prosecutor from 2004 to 2009. In 2009, he was appointed as the 37th Prosecutor General of Korea. As Prosecutor General, Mr. Kim pioneered and directed major reforms on Korean prosecution service to meet global standards. He also spearheaded the fight against corruption in Korea.

As the Vice President and an Executive Committee Member of the International Association of Prosecutors (IAP) from 2008 to 2011, he facilitated cooperation and friendship among prosecutors worldwide. Additionally, Mr. Kim proposed a Model Treaty titled *Asia-Pacific Convention on Cooperation in Criminal Justice*, to strengthen regional cooperation through 'direct contact and speedy response.' In 2011, he successfully hosted *the 4th World Summit for Prosecutors General, Attorneys General and Chief Prosecutors* in Seoul. Earlier in the same year, he was elected as an Honorary Member of IAP.

Not only did he dedicate his career as a prosecution service, but he also worked in Department of Justice as Deputy Minister, Assistant Minister for Legal Affairs and Director of International Legal Affairs. Mr. Kim actively participated in many international conferences and played the main role in numerous international negotiations on trade. He also founded Human Rights Bureau and served as the 1st Director-General of this new bureau in Ministry of Justice. He was engaged in many legislative activities; initiating enactment of Crime Victim Protection Act, Arbitration Act and Overseas Koreans Act; working on major amendment of civil and commercial laws for social advancement. Mr. Kim served as a diplomat, as Legal Attaché at the Embassy of Korea in the U.S. from 1994 to 1997.

Mr. Kim received his Bachelor of Law in 1979 from Seoul National University. After passing Judicial Exam, he completed training at Judicial Research and Training Institute in 1981. He also studied in the U.S. as a visiting scholar at the University of Michigan Law School from 1988 to 1989. During that time, he conducted research on organized crime and later published his findings in *The Justice* in 1991. He also attended U.S. Trade Law Program at Columbia University Law School in 1989.

After completing his term as Prosecutor General in 2011, Mr. Kim went to the U.S. again, this time to the University of Illinois Law College as a visiting scholar. There he completed his research for this book, based on his ten year-lectures on transnational crime. He gave a presentation on this topic at the University of Chicago Law School as well as at UIUC.

In 2012, Mr. Kim was awarded Order of Service Merit (Blue Stripes) from the Government of Korea, the highest honor for contribution to public service for thirty years. Mr. Kim is a dedicated husband, father, and grandfather living in Seoul. He enjoys clay modeling, cycling and playing the trumpet during his free time.

joongyukim@gmail.com +82-10-4901-3201

Cheol-Kyu Hwang

Cheol-Kyu Hwang has been serving as a prosecutor for twenty years. He is currently the Chief of Ansan Branch, Suwon District Prosecutors' Office, in Korea.

Mr. Hwang received his Bachelor of Laws in 1987 from Seoul National University and completed training at the Judicial Research & Training Institute (JRTI) in 1990. He obtained the LL.M. at George Washington University in 1998. He received his Ph.D. at the Graduate School of Law of Hanyang University in 2009. He is a member of the New York Bar.

From 2001 to 2003, He served as a Legal Counselor at the Permanent Mission of Korea to the UN. He participated in the consultation for establishing the International Criminal Court (ICC) as well as in the international legislation process of UNCITRAL. Between 2003 and 2006, as a Professor at the JRTI, he taught courses for the lawyer-candidates, including international criminal law. From 2006 to 2008, as the Director of International Criminal Affairs Division at the Ministry of Justice, he has dealt with various transnational crimes. He was also in charge of domestic legislation of the ICC Rome Statute and of the UN Convention against Corruption.

In 2010, Mr. Hwang was appointed as the Chief of International Cooperation Center at the Supreme Prosecutors' Office for practicing the 'direct contact and speedy response' of international cooperation and drafting the related Model Treaty. He took charge of the Task Force for preparation of *the 4th World Summit for Prosecutors General, Attorneys General and Chief Prosecutors* in 2011. He has been an Executive Committee Member of International Association of Prosecutors (IAP) since 2011.

hckslj93@gmail.com +82-10-7108-3198